D0310148

DAVID GOWER
With Time To Spare

'One aspect I enjoyed at Lord's during my 82 in the Second Test, 1979, was playing against Bishen Bedi. In county cricket previously Bish had never had any trouble with me and so it was pleasant to get revenge, depositing him over the ropes at square leg. Here the sweep is more controlled — along the ground, but worth only one to deep square. The ball was obviously pitching outside leg stump and turning further down the slope, as one can see by the wicketkeeper's hands, and so the shot carries with it minimal risk of dismissal, unless hit in the air. Viswanath is the gully fielder, perhaps hoping for a thick edge from the ball that goes on with the arm. There is no way that he is expected to catch anything from a forcing shot in his direction.'

DAVID GOWER

With Time To Spare

David Gower & Alan Lee

Ward Lock Limited London

'By the time this was taken at the Fourth Test at the Oval 1979, the wheel of fortune had turned against me. After successive ducks, one at Headingley and one in the first innings at the Oval, both lbw Kapil Dev, I again went cheaply – c. Reddy b. Bedi 7, attempting a late cut and managing only a thin bottom edge. Viswanath is the slip.'

The authors and publishers would like to thank Patrick Eagar for the photographs on pages 18, 20, 46/47, 78/79, 92, 96 and 100 and Adrian Murrell/ All Sport for all the others.

© David Gower Promotions 1980

First published in Great Britain in 1980 by Ward Lock Limited, 116 Baker Street, London W1M2BB, a Pentos Company.

House Editor Gillian Freeman

Designed by Chris Walker

Text filmset in 10/12 Times

Printed and bound in Great Britain by Butler & Tanner Ltd, Frome and London

British Library Cataloguing in Publication Data

Gower, David
    David Gower.
    1. Gower, David
    2. Cricket players – England – Biography
    I. Lee, Alan
    796.358′092′4   GV915.G/
    ISBN 0–7063–5928–3

Contents

*Leicestershire County Cricket Club (1978). The
section of the pavilion in the background has since
been developed, kitchens and indoor nets
redesigned. Players left to right. Back row:
M. Schepens, G. Parsons, P. Newman, L. B. Taylor.
K. Shuttleworth, P. B. Clift, D. I. Gower. N. E.
Briers, N. G. B. Cook, P. Booth, J. F. Steele.
Front row: J. C. Balderstone, C. T. Spencer,
R. W. Tolchard, B. F. Davison, C. Palmer
(Chairman), R. Illingworth, F. M. Turner
(Secretary/Manager), K. Higgs, J. Birkenshaw,
B. Dudleston, A. Ward.*

1. The County Scene

The first time David Gower set foot on a first-class cricket ground, he did something spectacular, and then departed. This was, perhaps, to be his style for a number of years. Boundless natural talent was always within him, but consistency was more elusive.

He was twelfth man for a Championship game at Worcester, early in the 1975 season. When his chance came to field, he was posted at backward short leg – an unusual place to find him these days – and almost immediately took off to his left to hold a stunning, one-handed catch. Before long, of course, he was relieved of his duties, and his only further part in the match was a spell fielding for the opposition, which was a common occurrence in his unglamorous days as a regular substitute.

The mystery, to many people, is that Gower should be playing for Leicestershire at all. He was, after all, they point out, born in Tunbridge Wells and educated in Canterbury, so Kent must surely have been the natural county to secure his services. Oddly, the fact of the matter is that Kent never made an approach to Gower, nor he one to them, and by the time he finished his schooling, his family had moved to Loughborough. For as long as Mike Turner has been their secretary-manager, Leicestershire have not been a county to allow talent to slip through their fingers, and it was purely a matter of time before the invitation came to play in the Club and Ground XI.

A phone call from Turner to Gower's mother secured his services for that particular minor fixture, and the upward progression was inevitable. In 1974, he played three Under-25 matches and three games in Leicester's second team, under the watchful eyes of Maurice Hallam and Terry Spencer, the seasoned players in charge of the county's young blood.

Without transport of his own, Gower was ferried to and from matches by his mother. His involvement ended there; he was not part of the staff, so he was not expected to train or practice with them. In between his county engagements, he just went on playing club cricket for Loughborough. All that changed the following summer. Gower was taken onto the playing staff and, on April 1st 1975, he celebrated his 18th birthday by reporting for pre-season training at Grace Road.

This was the year when Leicestershire won the County Championship for the first time in their history of almost 100 years. But Gower, still finishing his final year at King's College, took little part until the last third of the season. He made his Championship debut against Lancashire at Blackpool and began his career with a 32 which started sketchily – 'my first two scoring shots were edged drives which went between first and second slip' – but developed into fluency until, ironically, he skied a catch to mid-on off Ken Shuttleworth, the seam bowler who was to become a team-mate at Leicester within two years.

In truth, he played only a walk-on part in the county's triumph of that year, but the involvement was undoubtedly good for his cricket and his maturing sense of humour.

'I was a very shy person when I joined Leicester. It would be true to say that my cricket was more confident than my personality. I said little, and took time to make new friends. Probably the first person who I thought of as a friend was Mick Norman, who was playing his final season in the side and seemed to take a great interest in me. He took

On the charge during an innings of 85 not out against Northants at Leicester on a turning wicket. In fact that was debatable. The first ball I received turned alarmingly past the outside edge, but afterwards only comparatively few did anything similar. I still enjoyed the contest against their two off-spinners, Peter Willey and Richard Williams. Studying this effort of mine are the wicketkeeper, George Sharp, Jim Yardley and Allan Lamb. Allan Lamb scored a big hundred in the first innings and Jim Yardley gave me two chances in this game at backward point, both well struck, both diving catches, which gave me a lot of pleasure even if he did not share it initially.

time to advise and coach me, and I appreciated that. There were two players of similar age to me on the staff, in Martin Schepens and John Smith, and it was natural that we should start going around together. Gradually, I began to come out of my shell, and by the time I joined the first-team towards the end of the season, I felt far more confident about things.'

Confident enough, in fact, to include a gin and tonic among the orange squashes when he brought out the drinks as twelfth man during one Championship game, and to slip it to captain Ray Illingworth. Gower was twelfth man again at Chesterfield for the final match of the season, when the title was secured in mid-game and Leicester went

on to win in cavalier style. That evening, he was pouring champagne for everyone.

'It was great experience for me to be involved with a really successful side so early in my career, and with players who could teach me such a lot about the game. I remember, towards the end of that summer, that two players seemed to be doing everything. Norman McVicker and Garth McKenzie were both in the side for their seam bowling, but as well as bowling teams out, they were carrying us through by scoring most of the runs as well. They both retired at the end of that season, and left a big hole in the side, on and off the field. Norman was always a very amusing man with a fund of stories to tell, and although Garth was basically

Cautious defence against Northants against a good-length ball. I have pushed forward with as dead a bat as possible and the ball has slid harmlessly to the two close fielders, Allan Lamb and Jim Yardley. George Sharp is the wicketkeeper and Jim Watts the distant fielder.

9

that rarity – the quiet, modest Australian – he was so impressive in everything he did that we all respected him greatly.

'Illy, as ever, was the dominant personality of the side in his own unique fashion, but there were a number of characters. Jack Birkenshaw, another of our imported Yorkshiremen, was a livewire in the dressing-room, a very funny man, and I soon struck up a friendship with Brian Davison, the Rhodesian, whose wild man image was beginning to wane. Everyone played well that year and the side was not often changed, which bred a very intimate team spirit. Although I was the new boy, the young upstart if you like, I had no problems with acceptance and I found it a lot of fun adjusting to the routine of travelling with a county team.'

It was in 1975 that Gower acquired his own transport ... a 15-year-old Ford Anglia which had once belonged to his mother. It did not have much longer to live:

'That car had been brought back from East Africa by my parents, lovingly tended all the way home to Leicestershire. But I had it for only three months before I rolled it into a ditch at Narborough on my way home one night. The car and the hedge were both more badly hurt than I was!

'My next car was a Mini of a similar vintage, and that had an even shorter existence in my hands. Within a week, the engine blew up and that was the end of that. Nowadays, like most other county players, I have a car sponsored by a local dealer, which takes a lot of the worry out of the travelling. A county player has to cover thousands of miles every year, and there is nothing worse than breaking down in some inaccessible spot on a Friday night trip from Manchester to Southampton! I

A thoughtful moment. 'Have I shaved this week?' The keeper is Roger Tolchard my Leicester teammate and former 'landlord' who looks as if his benefit year might be on his mind as well as the game. His pads incorporate a newish idea for wicketkeeping. The top flaps, which only really get in the way, are omitted. We nicknamed these the 'magi-pads' at Leicester as every time the ball hit Tolly's it rebounded onto the stumps – useful for more than one stumping!

used to enjoy driving but there are times now when it can be a dreadful bind. With the John Player League on a Sunday often requiring a hectic drive on a Saturday night and a return trip 24 hours later, there is not much fun involved in cricket motoring.

'Generally, I would rather drive myself than be driven. I get tired at the wheel, but being a passenger is just boring and I find that even worse. When I am playing for Leicester, we share the driving around and I am often in someone else's car, but if I'm in my own, I will have the radio or a tape on almost constantly. It is a release from the tedium and helps me to retain concentration on some of the really long trips, when all I can think of is getting there in the shortest possible time.

'I believe I get on well enough with every member of the side. There is no ostracising, and only the odd, inevitable personality clash which will occasionally afflict every society in which people are thrown together for long periods at a time. But the person I am probably closest to is Roger Tolchard, whose flat I shared for two years before I moved into one of my own.

'The son rarely leaves home without some misgivings from the family, and that was certainly my experience. I was looking to move out, not because I was unhappy but because, like every other lad of my age, I was seeking greater independence. I was not rebellious and I did not want any unpleasantness – I just wanted everyone to be happy about my decision. After a good deal of discussions at home, I finally moved in with Tolly at the start of the 1977 season, by which time I was positively full-time on the Leicester staff.

'University had just not worked out. Some people it suits, some it does not, and I am afraid that by that stage, I had decided my future lay in cricket rather than any academic pursuit. I left London University before the end of my planned first year, and drove straight to Worcester. Several of the side had been injured in their previous match, so I was rushed straight into a Benson and Hedges Cup quarter-final. Unfortunately, that little story did not have the Boys' Own ending – we lost.

'The Worcester game, however, was the start of an unbroken spell of six weeks in the first team, which ended with my first county century – 102 not out against Middlesex at Lord's. Following that, I flew off to the West Indies for a short tour with

England Young Cricketers, returning only in time for the final week of the 1976 season and a defeat at Taunton, where we had needed to win to finish in the top-three prize money.

'My globe-trotting that year continued with a three-week trip to Canada, playing for Derrick Robins' XI, but I was brought back to earth in October when I actually had to do a job of work. You could say I was a deputy clerk in charge of teas. I worked at Bostik in Leicester, in the traffic office, and did everything from printing labels to driving the company vans and stacking tins in the warehouse. I never found it hard work, but I thought my incentive for doing things fast would be to put my feet up and have a longer break. Instead, I was regularly given a rollocking for lazing about. I was grateful enough for the job with Bostik, generous sponsors at Grace Road, but was not unhappy when the cricket season arrived.

'We won the John Player League that year, and I established myself in the side. The daily grind of ground-hotel-bar-meal-sleep-ground which has apparently driven the likes of Barry Richards to distraction was all new to me, and I loved it. Up to that point, most of my time had been spent in school and university accommodation, so the hotels at which we stayed on away trips were relatively luxurious.

'I was seeing places I had never seen before, and meeting new people all the time. Now, perhaps, the original novelty has gone and I can understand, if not exactly appreciate, how the older players can sometimes become cynical about our way of life. The more time you spend away from home, the easier it is to become critical of hotels and meals, or irritable with others in the side. Fortunately, I have not seriously encountered these problems yet in my career, and I hope I never do. In every job, there must be some continuity, which can become tedium. But I would rather be inevitably bored in parts of a life that I love, than in some other situation ... in an office, factory or coalmine.

'Playing cricket for a living has an aura of glamour attached, which means you will meet hundreds of people, dozens of whom you may not want to. It is all too simple to become a cynic about the existence. But I just think of the good things in the job which so easily outweigh the bad.'

2. Bachelor Life

If, like me, you have had a bachelor existence in which the washing-up multiplies into a china mountain, dirty clothes fester on the bedroom chair and the closest thing to cooking dinner at home is re-heating the chop suey from the chinese take-away, you will be relieved by the following piece of news. David Gower, precociously talented crick-eter though he may be, is as disorganised as the rest of us when it comes to domestic life.

The evidence is given by Roger Tolchard, Leices-tershire and England team-mate of Gower, and his long-suffering landlord for two summers. 'He has a nasty habit of hanging his shirts on the floor and leaving me to pick them up behind him,' was Tol-chard's testimony to the tenant who has now moved out – but not far. Gower these days has his own flat, separated from Tolchard's by just two floors of a pleasant court on the outskirts of Leicester.

Like most young men of his age, David was keen to set out on his own, and he enjoys the indepen-dence of living alone. Being a sociable creature, however, he has also experienced the vicious circle that goes with a solitary existence. 'If I come home thinking that, for once, I will have a quiet night at home, I very quickly get bored with my own com-pany. I like to have people around me and I never enjoy the idea of an evening spent alone, followed by an early night – yet I know that occasionally, it will do me good.'

Not surprisingly, the domestic chores of the single man's life fall heavily on Gower's shoulders. Washing up, he confesses, often has to wait for a day or two – 'but it never amounts to more than a plate and a couple of saucepans due to the limits of my cooking ability' – and, for clothes washing,

he relies on the push-button efficiency of the laun-derette, where he can often be seen occupying his early-evening time after a day of county cricket.

When he cooks for himself, the house speciality is omelettes. 'I like herbs and spices in omelettes – but I probably enjoy them so much because they are so easy to do! I am quite good at mashed pota-toes, too, but they are not often on the menu because I can never be bothered to peel them first. In terms of experimenting, I have restricted myself to attempts to cook chips without burning the place down, after my first unfortunate effort when I managed to fill the whole flat with thick, acrid smoke.'

Gower is not among the many devotees of the Chinese take-away. He has, he admits, eaten Chinese food but is in no hurry to repeat the experi-ence. 'I will do anything to avoid it. The thought of Chinese food appals me. If I do bring hot food back to the flat, it will often be doner kebabs from a very good Greek place in Leicester ... which is strange, because I am not fond of Greek food, either, on the whole.

'For someone living alone, it is so much easier to eat out than to mess about cooking just for one, so it is something I do a great deal. If I am going to a restaurant, I will generally choose English food, and almost invariably meat dishes. I love roasts and steaks, and I am very much one for the main course. If I can eat enough of that, then the sweets and cheeses do not really concern me. Formal dinners are not my scene. I enjoy res-taurants which have an intimate atmosphere, where you can enjoy yourself without worrying too much about what the elderly couple on the next table think of you.

Relaxing on the balcony at Leicester with the camera – one of my favourite hobbies. I am not sure if I would have had that grin on my face if I had known Adrian Murrell was looking up with his camera – or perhaps Brian Davison, glancing suspiciously under the bottom rail, was doing more than meets the eye!

'Away from English menus, I will eat most European food, and the occasional Indian curry, although anything too hot will instantly turn me off. One of my favourite dishes, which is not easy to find in England, is Malay satay, which I feasted on almost daily while I was in Singapore.

'I am one of those who considers eating to be among the great pleasures of life, especially if it is accompanied by a bottle of decent white wine, possibly a Pouilly Fuissé or a German wine, to which I am particularly partial. Many cricketers are apt to drink a good deal of beer, but although I like it in moderation, I find I feel very bloated if I stay on pints all evening. Instead, I might drink a little rum – I got something of a name for it after touring the West Indies with Young England – or probably wine. To finish a meal, there can be nothing better than a glass of good port.

'Leicestershire's players were invited to a wine and cheese party at the home of Lord Crawshaw, in aid of Roger Tolchard's benefit, and as my interest in port was beginning to flourish, I successfully bid for a bottle of Croft '45 in the auction. It is currently under my kitchen sink, awaiting the correct occasion for me to consume it!'

Music plays a significant part in Gower's life, but not in the fashion common to people of his era. Until the winter tour of 1979–80 he had never attended a rock or pop concert, but he had been to a good number of classical concerts.

'Classical music has always been in my family. My grandmother was a very good pianist, and her interest was passed on to my mother. When I was at school, there was a regular end-of-term drama week, which invariably included a symphony concert. I hardly missed one. I like watching the Proms – and not just the last night – and I have a lot of classics in my record collection, including a lot of Bach, Handel, Sibelius, Brahms, Tchaikovsky and Beethoven. If ever I am alone and feeling really down, then I will probably put a piece of classical music on the stereo.

'This should not sound as if I am against contemporary music. The majority of my records are what the disc-jockeys call soft rock, from groups such as Supertramp and Genesis and singer-songwriters like Al Stewart and Gerry Rafferty. The lyrics of any record are not important to me, although I can identify with the songs that these people write.

Stewart, in particular, associates a lot of his music with history, which is a subject I have always enjoyed and still have a wish to re-read at some stage. I have listened to the heavy rock bands and also to new-wave, but I can find nothing for me in it. There is, in my view, no musical value in the punk songs – but then, that is probably because I don't go for the brash, belligerent messages behind the songs.'

On a typical quiet night alone, Gower will be found propped up in bed, the stereo system playing music by Supertramp at a suitably powerful volume, while he reads either a satirical magazine or one of the Brant Parker and Johnny Hart books of cartoons, featuring the Wizard of Id.

'I find cartoons like these delightfully dry, good for late night reading. I usually buy *Time* magazine, but not for its political content, and I suppose *Punch* is my favourite magazine; I prefer it to the less subtle satirism of *Private Eye*. If I read books at home, they are liable to be light, perhaps by Wilbur Smith, or occasionally the more complex spy novels of John Le Carré.'

The typical morning at home is not so tranquil. Not being among the world's most willing risers, Gower is one of those who will leave the evil moment until it can be postponed no longer, then cram everything into the shortest possible time.

Breakfast, if indeed there is time for it at all, will be a hurried affair and the washing up will generally wait. His dressing, as has been noticed on one or two occasions chronicled in this book, is not always precise first thing and one gets the impression that the cleaning lady who calls once a week is not left idle chez Gower.

On days off, he diversifies perhaps more than the average cricketer. A country boy by birth and upbringing, but a city lover periodically, by nature, his thriving spare-time interests of art, antiques and photography keep him nicely nomadic between the two.

'I am no expert at any of these, but I do have a desire to own nice paintings and antiques and to take good photographs. Dutch landscapes I find very appealing, and I am lucky to have an uncle who is a picture framer. At the moment, though, there are prints lying around the flat waiting for me to find the time and the skill to hang them.

'Old furniture is something else in which I am

developing an interest. I bought a mahogany dining table from a local antique shop – I tend to prefer dark woods – and I can often be found, browsing for bargains there. The problem is finding space in the flat for anything more.

'Photography is something in which I have long had a distant interest, to the extent of being fascinated by pictures of people, both old and new. I do not believe it is the sort of thing you can do at all satisfactorily with an instamatic, however, so up to now I have never taken a camera on any tours, whereas the majority of players do. I bought a Pentax camera in Singapore on my way home from the 1978–79 Australian trip, and I am still at the experimental stage. I enjoy catching people off guard and I will happily sit for long periods waiting for the right moment. I want to do it well, not just have a batch of meaningless snaps.'

That significant desire again: wanting to do things properly, snubbing anything that smacks of second best. Under the languid actions and lazy airs, it is that quietly prominent attitude which has taken Gower to the considerable achievements which his young career have already brought him. He reveals more about his thoughtful side when he talks of his love of the country, notably the Forest

He seems to have caught it – but can he believe it? Anyway, Tolly must have needed congratulating for something.

and the Stilton Cheese villages of Leicestershire, then immediately qualifies such romantic notions by emphasising how much he enjoys his visits to London.

'I am not the rural sort who could exist solely in quiet countryside. I seem to have a personality which craves the best of both worlds, and I am lucky in that I have them readily available. Within a few minutes drive of Leicester, there is plenty of pleasant countryside and there are times when I like nothing better than to go there, to one of the peaceful villages or to Rutland Water or Charnwood Forest, and so escape from the hustle of life. But, on the other hand, there are plenty of occasions when I feel more at home in the big city.

'London has a great fascination to me, not only because there is so much to do on the social side, but also because of its inhabitants. It would not bore me at all to spend some time standing in one of the busier centres, like Leicester Square, just studying people and the way they behave.'

Gower's deeper traits do not, thankfully, carry him far from his basic love of life. The wine, women and song syndrome present in most of us has certainly not passed him by: he likes a drink, slim, beautiful girls and music – and not necessarily in that order. If his bachelor life is not neatly ordered, then it certainly contains the ingredients that many see in his cricket. As he says: 'At home, I can often feel casual, apathetic and disorganised; then suddenly, I will get the urge to put everything right, and I will have a mad clear-up.'

3. Batting and Batsmen

It is a fact of life that most cricketers bat right-handed. More fascinating is why a proportion, including David Gower, are different. Gower himself is a confusion to all theories. Although he bats left-handed, he bowls and throws with his right arm, writes with his right hand, and plays golf and hockey right-handed. He even kicks a football predominantly with his right foot.

'I remember that when I first picked up a bat, probably in the back garden, I naturally used it in the left-handed style. My father thought it was wrong and tried to change me, but my mother left me alone. Playing golf right-handed was more of necessity than design, because we did not possess any left-handed clubs, but it still feels more natural that way round. It might be significant that my earliest cricketing heroes were Graeme Pollock and Gary Sobers, both of them left-handed batsmen. I saw Pollock at Trent Bridge in 1965, and in later years at Port Elizabeth in South Africa. He made a hundred on both occasions. My lasting memory of Sobers is again of a match at Nottingham, when he murdered everything England could bowl at him to make 70 very quickly.

'My family had such a long-standing interest in

One of my early idols – left-hander Graeme Pollock. I can remember watching him 'live' twice, once at Trent Bridge in a Test Match and once in Port Elizabeth. Both times he scored hundreds and kept this fan. Admittedly the first time I was quite young (1965) and probably did not watch with as much appreciation as later.

cricket that it was always part of my life to watch the game and enjoy it, at all levels, but from an early age, the memories of these two players are the strongest. To be frank, I could not say how much they influenced the way I bat. They are very different players: Pollock was robust, muscular and always hit the ball with great freedom and power; Sobers was a wristier, more elegant batsman, but certainly not short of strength. The only thing about them that I can say, with any certainty, fashioned my own career is that they kept hitting the ball to the boundary and patently disliked being tied down. I would rather watch that sort of player, than a technical accumulator. I also try to bat their way.'

Just like every other strokeplayer, Gower has learned that you cannot please everybody all the time. They will love you for your belligerence and your boundaries, curse you as a fool for the occasional abberation which gets you out. Gower has often been criticised as a player who takes things too lazily, in whom confidence becomes arrogance and so casualness. It is an allegation he does not entirely refute.

'There ARE days when I feel lazy, when I know I have no adrenalin flowing and it is difficult to motivate myself. But there are also times when I have read a newspaper report of our game and found myself accused of casualness – and it has come as a complete shock, because I was not aware of it at the time.

'If you are the sort of player who likes to go for shots, you are going to get criticised now and again. It is as simple as that. For instance, I might play a delicate shot outside off-stump and drift the ball past the slips for four through third man. The

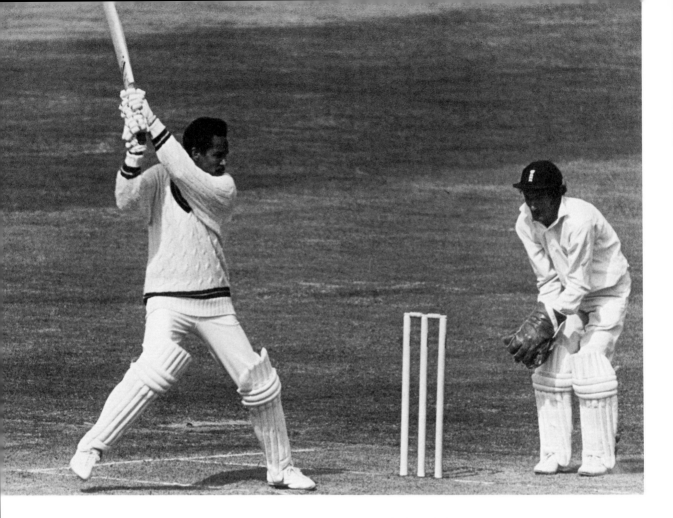

Sir Garfield Sobers, another one of my idols, mostly through television. I did however, watch him at Trent Bridge one day when he carved 77 in about 40 minutes, mostly square on the off-side, nearly always piercing the field on the edge.

crowd think it is marvellous. A few deliveries later I might play the same shot to a similar ball, nick it and get caught behind. The crowd will tell me I am a lazy young idiot.

'Sometimes, I feel foolish myself after such dismissals, not because I have been lazy as such, but because I did not consider every possibility. It is very dangerous to glibly reel off the same stroke to what looks an identical delivery to one I have just hit for four. I should be alert to the chance of it being a faster ball, or bowled from a wider angle ... any slight variation which could mean the difference between another acclaimed boundary and an unpleasant walk back to the insults.

'I know I am an instinctive batsman and that will never change. Once I have played myself in, I play strokes naturally. My sort of player is always giving the bowlers a chance, more of a chance than someone like Boycott would give them. But I would not think of playing any other way.

'Contrary to the view of many people, I never look to go in and play strokes from the off – never,

that is, unless the situation is such to demand it, as it was in the Prudential World Cup Final of 1979. In normal circumstances, I much prefer to start slowly, get off the mark with a few singles here and there, and develop my innings until I am playing strokes with assurance. It may be pure superstition, but if I have gone in and hit the first couple for fours, I have usually felt uneasy. All too often, that has been the sign for a dismissal when I have made only 10 or 12; the days when I have hit the ball cleanly from the start and gone on to a big score have been rare indeed.

'Number four or five is my customary place, and my best place. Batting there gives me the opportunity to assess conditions before I go out. One can never judge accurately from the pavilion, but it is possible to get some idea of the pace of the wicket, how much movement the bowlers are achieving, and which of the bowlers is having a good day.

'My priority on going in is to survive the first ball and, in general, I will not look to score from it. After that, there is a period of mind-reading

Viv Richards, World Cup Final, 1979. He and Collis King virtually won the game between them, though Viv needed a little luck early on to survive. Certainly most sides would hope to dismiss him early on, with the only alternative sometimes being to carry on bowling till he gets bored with batting. Powerful and strongest playing to leg.

attempts, when I try to decide which way the bowler might swing the ball, and if he is likely to drop it short or keep it up. You should never, of course, decide on a stroke until the ball has been delivered, but such conjecture helps keep me on my toes.

'When I first joined Leicestershire, I was an almost exclusively front-foot player, who loved to drive through the covers. Nowadays, I have adapted my game to the extent that I play almost all pace bowling off the back foot. Playing abroad has had a good deal to do with this change. On the quicker wickets of Australia, for instance, it is asking for trouble to keep coming forward to anyone of real pace, such as Rodney Hogg. I feel safer and more balanced on the back foot, and I have developed the pull shot and a reasonable back-foot drive.

'I hit the ball in the air a fair amount. Some people would say too often. There are times when it is designed, but more often it is unwitting. Again, those batsmen who play as I do are likely to play more shots off the ground than the more defensive batsmen. It only needs a fractional failing in timing, and a powerfully-struck shot will go up. If you are lucky, it will find a gap. If you are not, it will be caught, sometimes in the most unfortunate manner.

'During a John Player League match at Old Trafford in 1979, I had scored a few runs quickly – a bad sign, again – when I drove Bob Ratcliffe, on the up and off the meat of the bat. Frank Hayes, the Lancashire captain, was standing quite close at extra-cover and had no time either to get his hands up to the ball, or get out of the way! The ball thudded into his chest and he caught it on the rebound. Some people would certainly say that I was dicing with death by playing that sort of shot, but to my mind I was still rather unlucky to get out. I take chances, especially in limited-over games, and if I hit the ball cleanly I will more often than not get away with it.

'I am more a player of touch and timing than of strength, and timing is the one thing that nobody-can coach into a player. Everybody has some sort of timing, either good or bad, and with me the touch was natural.

'The strongest players, such as Ian Botham and Gordon Greenidge, do not need to rely solely upon timing. They can score a great deal of runs through their natural strength. But if I ever hit a ball out of the ground, it is chiefly through timing. I do not consider myself a weak person, but my wiry build dictates that I could never match the strength of a Botham.'

At the start of his first-class career, David was considered a better player of seam than spin. The experts at Leicester, Ray Illingworth prominent among them, rapidly sorted out his deficiencies against the turning ball and set to work on it. The result of that coaching, allied to the glut of pace that he has had to face more recently, has produced a change in his preferences, if not his strengths.

'I could not pretend that I am a great player of spin, even now, but I certainly feel more confident. I prefer facing the slow bowlers because they provide me with a technical challenge, as against the challenge of the pacemen which, these days, is dominated by courage.

'All the Leicestershire spinners helped me in my early days with the county. I was usually put in the spinners' net rather than the seamers' net and instructed on movement of feet, bat-pad techniques, etc. My early encounters with Bishen Bedi, for one, were rather embarrassing, as he used to get me out within two or three balls. I was unfamiliar with his flight and variations, and more than once found myself caught in no man's land – neither forward to the pitch of the ball, nor back on the stumps to play it with the spin.

'Perhaps, by 1979, he was not quite the bowler he had been, but I was nevertheless pleased to take runs off him in two of our Tests against India. During that season, I also made runs against Northants' off-spinners, Peter Willey and Richard Williams, after the first ball to me had turned inches past the bat. I saw that as a test of technique, put my head down and did not get out, although it must be said that only comparatively few balls misbehaved as badly as the first one.

Barry Richards is always a pleasure to watch and certainly at the top of my list of batsmen. Despite his all too obvious ability, he has been accused of merely turning it on when he wanted. I wish that others of us could make hundreds at will.

DAVID GOWER

Above Gordon Greenidge seen here during the Courage Challenge 1979, where his power made him an early favourite. Unfortunately for him Clive Lloyd just defeated him in one of the best contests of the competition.
Opposite Clive Lloyd batting in the Courage Challenge Final 1979, where he, unfortunately for me, took complete control and hardly ever looked like getting out. At least I was in a good position to watch it all.

'On another significant occasion, I scored 98 against Phil Edmonds and John Emburey of Middlesex, in a Championship match at Leicester. Eventually, I probably got myself out through complacency. I had never before been out in either the eighties or nineties and, subconsciously, I think I had decided that the century was there for the taking.'

As the subject of fast bowlers arose, I put to Gower the question which occasionally hovers in the mind of every journalist, and which is carefully diverted by almost every batsman. Has any bowler ever frightened him?

'No player likes to admit to being petrified at the crease, and I have certainly never been frozen with fear. However, when bowlers consistently aim for the body, things become slightly unpleasant.

'Any bowler can worry you if he is firing well, and some have the reputations to worry you when they are not. There are two ways of treating a repu-

24

tation. One can either dismiss it, bare the teeth and silently tell oneself that this guy is not going to get ME out, or one can respect it, watch the bowler more closely and build confidence by survival at the crease.

'Joel Garner is a man I shall always respect whenever I face him. But, by the end of 1979, I had somehow only batted against him for three deliveries. They came during the World Cup Final, when all normal reason was lost to a wild chase for runs, and Joel took out my off stump as I tried to glide him to third man. His impact, however, has been so immense that most batsmen must now regard him with very healthy respect.

'Of the other quick men who have bowled against me, I have been most concerned by Wayne Daniel, who is genuinely fast when his mood is right, and Imran Khan, who angles the ball into you from wide of the crease and consistently drops it short so that it chases your body. Hogg commanded respect throughout my first Australian tour. He bowled short, sharp spells, mixing a regular fast-medium pace with the occasional very quick delivery. His greatest quality was bowling straight, because he had reasoned that if he bowled short, we would duck, and if he bowled wide, we would leave them alone. Sensible thinking, that.'

Pollock and Sobers we have mentioned, as the early batting idols of the young Gower. But among his contemporaries, those he has played with or against, he selects six greats ... with two standing out above the rest.

Zaheer Abbas (Gloucestershire and Pakistan). A very fine strokemaker who seems to score most of his runs on the off-side, however many fielders occupy that area.

'The two Richards, Viv and Barry, must be the finest players of my time. Like Pollock and Sobers, their styles are contrasting, but they both have the great hallmark of playing each stroke with the impression of having time to spare. Barry is the artist of the two, a graceful player with marvellous timing and every conceivable shot. I watched him make the last 80 of a double-century at Perth during the first season of World Series Cricket, and he was so good that some of the best and fastest bowlers in the world were visibly destroyed and bewildered. I had the dubious privilege of being closer to the action for his century for Hampshire against Leicestershire in a televised John Player League match a few years ago. For much of his amazing innings, I was fielding at extra-cover, and it was impossible to count the amount of times the ball went past me, to either side, or over the top of me ... very seldom at me. He even made Ray Illingworth look a novice that day, stepping outside leg stump to drive him over long-off for six, then gliding the next ball delicately through fine-leg. It was surely one of the greatest innings of recent years, with Barry inspired, as ever, by the cameras.

'Viv was starting to come to fame when I began playing, and his great years followed very quickly. He hits the ball with thunderous power, anywhere on the ground, and I particularly remember a century he scored against us at Leicester in 1977. As I recall, Alan Ward, who is not the slowest bowler in the world, bowled one over in which every ball disappeared for runs. It simply did not matter where he pitched it, Viv would go through with the shot in that mighty arc.'

Gordon Greenidge, Clive Lloyd, Zaheer Abbas and Sunil Gavaskar complete Gower's half-dozen and he refuses an attempt to separate them. 'Once you reach that calibre, you are together on a plane above all the rest,' he says. There are many good judges who believe Gower is rising to those heights.

4. In the Field

There are two types of fielder appealing and exciting to the eye of the cricket spectator. One is the close catcher, brave, alert and skilful in the mould of a Simpson, Sobers or Mike Smith; the other is the outfielder, who will cover ground as if on wheels, stop the unstoppable and return over the bails from more than fifty yards. Colin Bland of South Africa was perhaps the archetype, Clive Lloyd almost as brilliant. But England are currently blessed with perhaps the most spectacular pairing of outfielders for some years in Derek Randall and David Gower.

Sharing the duties at cover and mid-wicket, Randall and Gower effectively stifle the batsmen's chances of the quickly-taken single. Many have tried and many have died in the attempt for, in addition to speed, certainty of hand and impeccable balance, both have an awesome record when it comes to a shy at the stumps. They are, however, vastly different to watch. Although Gower indulges in an occasional extrovert gesture – he once gathered up a balloon which had blown onto the field during a Leeds Test and fielded for some minutes with it stuffed inside his sweater – he is largely unobtrusive. The sort one only notices when he does something stunning to grab the attention.

Randall performs like the screwed-up bundle of nervous energy that he undoubtedly is. He jaunts back to his mark, swapping gestures and advice with the crowd and perhaps, in his more outrageous moments, turning a handstand or two or, throwing his cap in the air and catching it on his head again. Then he bounds in, hopping, skipping and striding in a manner that it would take a talented comedian to imitate.

In their own private ways, however, they are both striving for the most elusive and important quality in any great fielder – prolonged and unbroken concentration.

There is not a cricketer alive who, if pressed for the truth, will not confess to the odd misfield or missed catch caused by a temporary loss of alertness – the exception would be a superhuman. The best fielders are simply those who, in addition to their natural abilities, are able to concentrate the longest.

Gower makes no claims on superman status. In everyday life, he is a man whose concentration is not readily held, which leads me to wonder whether he could ever be an outstanding success at slip, for instance, where momentary loss of attention can be more crucial than in his present residential position. Against this, he has developed his gifts conscientiously, and combines a brilliant eye with fluid movements and a generally safe pair of hands. He will freely admit, however, that there are times when his mind wanders elsewhere ...

'When I first go out to field, early in the morning, my only enemy is sleepiness. Generally, this is the

Most of my time in the World Cup was spent spectating in one form or another. Here Derek Randall has brilliantly run out Gordon Greenidge in the final, and his momentum carried him on towards me where I caught him in mid leap. I have wondered since what would have happened had I not caught him. 'Both' has arrived already and 'Ned' Larkins, playing in his second international game is on his way. He, like myself, sadly did not sparkle with the bat in this tournament.

easiest time to concentrate. The anticipation and uncertainty keep me naturally alert and the first 20 minutes or so disappear very rapidly. Thereafter, the degree of difficulty in maintaining full concentration depends on the direction the game is taking. If the batsmen are on top and the ball is regularly being hit into my area, I feel involved and aware. Similarly, if wickets are falling, there is the element of enjoyment, which insures against lapses. But if the batsmen are blocking, little or nothing comes my way and yet wickets remain intact, I quite frequently find myself slipping. The signs are simple. I will look around the crowd for familiar faces, glance at the clock and wonder if there can really be another 90 minutes to lunch, curse myself for not having got up in time for breakfast or, just as likely, for forgetting to buy the eggs anyway.

'It is possible to doze off alone while everyone else is still on their toes. But it is much more likely that, in a flat period of play, most of the fielders around you will have lost their sharpness, too. It is usually a mistake – a misfield or a dropped catch – which wakes everyone up, and you are pretty unlucky if it happens to be yours.

'I can occasionally work out, quite suddenly, that things are slipping and I must pull myself together, but by far the easiest and best way out of a bad patch is to take a catch, or make a good stop. On the two occasions in first-class cricket when I have been allowed a spell of bowling, I have found the session of play slipping past far more quickly than usual. But on the other hand, I would not relish bowling 25 overs a day too often.

'Conversation in the field helps to keep you alert. When I am playing for Leicester, I often share the covers with Rhodesian, Brian Davison. He is a great chatter, Davo, and together we normally have a joke and a laugh, keeping each other going. If you are happy on the field, the chances are you will be alert, too.

'Fielding at cover for England, however, can be a lonely business. The field-placing tends to be more attacking in Test cricket, which means that the only people who get a chance of a chat are the wicketkeeper and slips. It's a different society there. If Derek Randall or I have something to say, we have to talk to ourselves – and 'Arkle' frequently does!

'Lots of people are eager to know what we all talk about when we get into clusters at the fall of each wicket. Sometimes, of course, we are discussing the strengths and weaknesses of the next batsman or the state of the pitch, or maybe a possible change of bowling. But just as often, cricket hardly merits a mention in the conversation. Females, food, drink, television will all be discussed, and that is not a bad thing – it gives us a breather and allows us a natural break in concentration, from which we are more likely to return refreshed.'

Fielding, to some cricketers, is a tedious chore to be endured between the more glamorous pursuits of batting and bowling. But Gower and Randall are living proof of the theory that it will be enjoyed very much more by someone who constantly aims to improve his standards.

'It was certainly a part of the game which I did not fully appreciate until I started playing at county level. But perhaps the first time I became aware of the thrill and value of outstanding fielding was when Paul Parker came to King's Canterbury as one of the MCC team, who played an annual fixture against us. Paul, who now plays for Sussex, is only a year older than me, but even then, when he was just 18, he was better than anyone I had ever played against – tremendously quick and with a great arm. I later played in second eleven cricket, by which time I had improved and was beginning to shake the lazy points out of my game. I was aware that fielding even at that level was a class above anything I had previously experienced.

'Ray Illingworth probably did as much to help my fielding as anyone. He would hold sessions in which he crucified us for being casual, and took us back to what he called "the ABC's of cricket". They included using two hands to pick up the ball whenever possible – at school, it had seemed "flash" to use only one hand, and I carried that attitude on to Leicester, where Illy rapidly drummed it out of me.

'Jack Birkenshaw, another of our spin bowlers at Leicester, is also a fanatic for fielding practices, and is still working to improve his own performances at the age of 39. It is that sort of attitude which inspires me to keep working on this part of the game.

'Overall, I have learned to enjoy fielding, but it is much easier to do so when I am fielding opposite someone like "Arkle". His brilliance gives me a

A damp morning's training at Leicester. On such days I would fully endorse the idea of training in tracksuits – surely a matter of commonsense. I for one, am not going to clean another set of whites merely because of one of these sessions. This method of practising slip catching is the same as we use in the England side and has the advantage of being enjoyable as well as functional. Roger Tolchard, at the back, underarms the ball to Brian Davison who then directs it towards the 'slips' – here myself, Les Taylor and Barry Dudleston. Curiously, none of us specialise in the slips, Les and Barry being mainly long-leg to mid-off men (Barry abandoned his specialist short-leg position years ago). Nevertheless, the practice is good for the reflexes and valuable to anyone who uses it.

One more that got away. Viswanath, the batsman, is particularly strong in this area square of the off-stump and just behind and Mike Brearley would usually employ me in a deep square gully position with an orthodox gully fielding in the position in which I am here. What I remember is that even with two gullies 'Vishy' still hit the ball very hard in that direction and did not go short of runs in the series. The umpire is Kenny Palmer.

challenge, a target to aim for, and we keep ourselves going with a competitive atmosphere. If he pulls off a great stop, then I want to produce one of my own.

'We have both gained something of a reputation for running people out with throws hitting the stumps direct. It is spectacular, and gives me a lot of satisfaction when it come off, but there is such a fine dividing line between success and failure that I feel luck plays a part here.

'I have sequences when I can't stop hitting the stumps, and then a baffling run when I keep missing. In Australia on the 1978-79 tour, Arkle was in a frustrating patch when he just could not hit the stumps, whereas I could do nothing wrong. But back in England, during the 1979 Prudential World Cup, I remember him throwing down the stumps four times, while I missed with every one of four attempts.

'It was in Australia that I developed an underarm throw which picked up a few victims at the non-striker's end. They kept taking singles to me, and I would pick the ball up on the run and basically roll it at the stumps. Again, it did not seem to work so much when I came back to England, apart from one occasion at Nottingham which gave me a lot of satisfaction.

'Almost on the stroke of lunch, the ball was pushed into the covers and the batsmen set off for a single. Everything was right, the angle, the speed of the ball and my pick-up. Sure enough, the under-arm throw hit its target, and the umpire's finger was raised. My comradely pleasure at this particular strike is simply explained – the man I had run out was Derek Randall!

'In the course of a season, though, I expect to miss the stumps as often as I hit them – and there will inevitably be times when a shy produces over-throws and the fielder looks a mug when another inch to one side would have made him a hero. A fickle game, this.'

Gower follows the classic style of cover fielders, with a variation or two of his own. He watches the bowler at the start of his run, walks in with him and times his approach to reach the area he wants to be as the ball is delivered. By that time, his eyes will be on the batsman.

'It is usually possible to assess the batsman's intention from the movement of his feet, and the pick-up of his bat. If he is rocking on to his back foot, and I am at cover, it may well be his aim to punch the ball square, in my direction. So, if I think he is attacking, I stop, spread my feet wide and balance myself ready to push off in either direction. Some fielders keep going in at pace, but you then have to set off in a curve to go after the ball, and a precious few yards may be lost.

'If the batsman is dropping the ball defensively in front of him, I keep going in, increasing my pace to cut off the chance of a pinched single.'

People tend to imagine that Gower must have been an outfielder all his life, that he must have been an athlete at school to develop his speed off the mark, and that much of his ability is so natural that it needs no practising. None of these things is true.

'At school, I was never thought of as being particularly quick over the ground, and in fact I tended to avoid athletics until my final year, when for some reason I cannot recall, I entered for the long jump in the school sports. During those years, I generally fielded at first slip. It was only when I began playing club cricket – in which it is traditional for the more senior players to occupy the slip places – that I was pushed out into the covers, and even when I joined Leicestershire, I told the second team captain that I was a slip fielder.

'My days in the close-catching positions were probably numbered after one weekend club match, for Loughborough at Leicester Ivanhoe. Fielding at cover and mid-wicket, I ran two men out, held a good catch and stopped everything. Word got back to Maurice Hallam, then the coach at Leicester, and I was marked down as a cover from that day on.

'Occasionally, I creep in at third or fourth slip for Leicester, or at gully for England, and I enjoy the change of angle and company. But it might have been fortunate that, throughout 1979, not one catch came my way in the close positions.

'The slips are always the most likely to put catches down, partly because the ball comes fast and at varying angles to test all reflexes, and partly through the frequency of chances in that region. But I have still managed my quota of embarrassing spills in the outfield positions.

'Probably the worst of all so far occurred in 1977 at Canterbury, when Jack Birkenshaw was bowling to Asif Iqbal, Kent's Pakistani Test cricketer and, at that stage, their captain. Asif went on the back foot to try and club a shorter ball through the on-side, but his shot was hopelessly mistimed and he uttered a fitting expletive as the ball just lobbed off his bat and looped gently towards me at cover.

'It is hard to explain just what goes through a fielder's mind when this sort of catch arrives, but in my case, I don't think I actually say to myself "this is easy". It never is. On this occasion, I closed my hands on the ball too soon, it bounced limply off the ends of my fingers and fell at my feet. I too, offered an expletive, similar to Asif's, who was by this time well on his way back to the pavilion and had to be recalled and told that "the silly young bugger's dropped it".

'Much more common in my type of position is a lapse in ground fielding. But the cause is almost always the same as that for a dropped catch – a temporary loss of concentration and the eyes taken off the ball too soon. As "Illy" never stopped telling us at Leicester, the basics are the most important things – use two hands not one, and watch the ball right into the hands.

'There are parts of fielding which can be practised, and other parts which develop naturally. My speed, for instance, has improved steadily over the years without my making conscious attempts to do

Adelaide, Fifth Test, last day, January 1979. Hughes c. Gower b. Hendrick 46. Australia began the final day with eight wickets intact and started well against the spinners, before Hendrick and Botham came on. Hendo bowled Yallop and then I caught Kim Hughes driving at backward point. At the time I had been thinking that I would like to do something dramatic and a diving catch suited me fine, so much so that I ended up like this, but thankfully not for too long. Others include Hendo, Both, Brearley and Gooch.

anything about it. But the fact that I play a lot of squash must have been beneficial to the short sprints which are so important.

'The fundamentals of running, picking up and throwing require a certain amount of co-ordination, and we practise this with a specific exercise in our pre-season training sessions. Someone stands with a bat and hits the ball to one side, calling the name of the player who must collect and return. It is then hit to the other side, and the same fielder has to repeat the operation possibly half a dozen times. Very tiring, but excellent practice.

'Throwing can be something of a mystery to me. I cannot explain why or when it is going to come out right. When I joined Leicester, my throw was usually strong enough to reach the wicketkeeper from the edge of the long boundary, but after injuring my shoulder a couple of years back, there are now times when it stiffens up so badly that I can barely throw 30 yards. When such problems arise, I have to change my style to whatever feels most comfortable.'

5. Nerves and Temper

The nerveless batsman. Unruffled, unflappable, the young man who plays without cares or inhibitions … all these things have been said or written about David Gower. All of them are untrue. I doubt whether the batsman without nerves has been invented, but if he has, the mould is not the subject of this book. Confident, certainly. Arrogant, sometimes. But always, there are the flutterings and the worries which afflict everyone who plays this game.

Gower's equable temperament is no myth. He certainly does possess a placid, easy-going nature which all the vagaries of periodical failure are hard pushed to upset. But even that 'cool cat' exterior, as Mike Brearley once called it, has occasionally cracked under stress. Flashes of temper may be rare in Gower, but they are not unknown.

One Sunday in 1979, he smashed down his stumps in an improbable tantrum, after being caught behind while playing for Leicestershire against the Indian tourists. The popular press seized upon the story, not because it was an unusual occurrence but because it was so unexpected in Gower. Weeks later, David still found it difficult to explain or justify such an irrational act.

'I had not been playing well and the team were struggling,' he recalled. 'So I saw my innings that day as having two major aims. With the First Test approaching, it was a chance for me to have a look at the Indian bowlers, sort out their strengths and weaknesses. And then, I wanted to play well to get the team out of trouble. The wicket was not good – there had been uneven bounce at Grace Road all season – so I was conscious of thinking about the short balls and the varying heights. But I was bobbing on, as we say at Leicester, without too many worries until I got myself out.

'It was a ball down the leg-side that did it – a ball to have a swish at, but not a ball to get you out. But I nicked it to the wicketkeeper and that was that. I wasn't worried by the decision, I knew I was out. But I felt suddenly and fiercely annoyed with myself for getting out in that way, and just for a few seconds I had the urge to hit something. The stumps were closest, so down they went.

'I would call it more a half-hearted swipe than a real slog at the stumps, but as soon as I made contact, three thoughts came into my mind. I knew it was not right, I knew it was an unusual spark of emotion in me … but primarily, I knew it had cheered me up. I went off the field at a march, with a smile on my face instead of slinking off sullenly.

'Of course, it is not the sort of thing I would want to make a habit of, nor would I encourage anyone else to try it. But I was fascinated by the cause and the result. It was a way of releasing pent-up tension – an unorthodox way, but a successful one, nonetheless. Most of our players thought it was funny, and the crowd were certainly amused. But Mike Turner ticked me off, and I can't say I blame him.'

If that incident smacked of the exhibitionist, something of which no-one who knows him could accuse Gower, then it only camouflages the moral involved. If David Gower gets annoyed, then the subject of his wrath is normally himself.

'I could count on the fingers of one hand the number of times I have been upset by another player on the field – and when it has happened, I have very seldom shown my feelings. But I often feel irritated at myself, either at my own shortcomings, or at just a silly lapse. It is much more common for me to show temper off the field, with

Above This delivery from Hogg was straight and just the right degree of shortness to be awkward – eventually making contact on the neck, without being too painful. Perhaps the most important result was to make me more determined not to get out to him and in fact he was taken off soon after. I was in the very early part of my innings then during the Second Test in Perth 1978, and did not have to worry about Hoggy again till the second new ball when I was nearer 80.

Opposite Rodney Hogg at Brisbane, First Test 1978–79, preying on the nerves of batsmen. He bowls most effectively by keeping the ball straight and up to the bat and was not averse to bowling a spattering of bouncers and using this ploy of going round the wicket and aiming into the body of the left-hander – keeps things interesting.

people who bother me in the street or the pub.' But that is another story.

For any batsman, the period before an innings is uncomfortable, even tortured. But when do the nerves begin to bite? Here, individuals vary; for Gower, it all starts as soon as he wakes up in the morning.

'I'm a reluctant riser, but whenever I do manage to get up early during the summer, I enjoy the first part of the morning. The period between six and nine is so often the best, crispest weather of the day. My first thoughts are usually concerned with the opposition for the day and, if I'm likely to be batting, then especially the particular bowlers. I will generally think about the wicket, wonder how it is going to play – all of which, I suppose, is my nervous system getting into gear.

World Cup 1979. Run out by Lance Cairns' throw from long-on. One of my more tragic misjudgements as Lance, with a strong arm, already had the ball in his hand when I slipped, turning back for the second. For some unknown reason I still carried on but remained a yard short despite the dive, when Jeremy Coney removed the bails. Lees is the wicketkeeper and Gooch the other batsman. It is Burgess leaping up to test the wind direction in the stratosphere.

'Breakfast is a meal which I enjoy, providing it is cooked for me. That must be a mark of my bachelor lack of domesticity, or maybe sheer laziness, but the last thing I want to face in the mornings is a collection of saucepans and frying pans to wash up. My normal choice would be a couple of fried eggs on toast, but, if I'm not in the cooking mood, I make do with cereal, toast, and then either tea or coffee. I find that, if I don't eat a reasonable breakfast, I suffer for it with hunger pains later in the day.

'The nerves are sometimes bad when I get to the ground, but they ease when I go through my exercise routine. This was initiated by Bernie Thomas, the England physio, and is invariably organised at Test matches. But I try to complete at least a proportion of the routines before any county day, especially those which stretch the vulnerable muscles in my groin, hamstring and throwing shoulder.

'I generally bat at number four or five these days, which gives me the benefit of time to assess the bowlers and the wicket. On occasions, however, this can be turned into a disadvantage – I am particularly reminded of the first match of the 1978–79 tour at Adelaide when I sat with my pads on watching Rodney Hogg bringing the ball up sharply off a length, and sending Clive Radley to hospital. Not good for the nerves.

'It has occurred to me that there is a strange anomaly about this game in that, so far as I am concerned, the more I have played and the greater my experience, the more I have suffered from nerves. Most people would assume that the reverse applies, but I believe that nerves are chiefly caused by two things – a fear of failure and an appreciation of the dangers. Neither disappears with experience, and although success may breed confidence, thus diminishing the failure phobia, my concern over injuries has only increased as I have witnessed, at close quarters, more and more such accidents to people close to me.

'On the day that I played my first Test innings for England, I was suffering from genuine jitters – the big-occasion wobbles which, when you analyse them, must come from this dreadful feeling that you may be ridiculed in front of so many people. It was also a fear of the unknown. But now, with a few Tests behind me, I am nervous before batting

for England more because I do know what to expect – and there are certain things which I don't relish.

'Whatever anyone may claim, no batsman likes facing fast, consistently short-pitched bowling, particularly on an untrustworthy wicket.

'In the early part of my career, I would always look to take on the quicks by standing up and hooking, or cutting. At that stage, I didn't think about being hit; playing the shot, or ducking when necessary, came very naturally.

'The match which brought home the dangers to me was my first meeting with the West Indies. Andy Roberts was comfortably the fastest bowler I had ever faced, and suddenly the physical risk became more apparent.

'A similar thing occurred in Australia on my first England tour. I was not making runs, and the fact that players had been hit on the head only increased the tension in my game. By the time the First Test arrived, I had decided to swallow pride and wear a helmet for the first time.

'The possibility of being hit is always in the back of the mind, however you might fight to get rid of it. But it is odd that on the occasions that I have been "skulled", it has not really hurt. Once, it even served to wake me up.

'We were playing Derbyshire at Leicester, and I was batting early in the morning session. Colin Tunnicliffe dropped one short and I ducked, but the ball failed to get up as much as I had expected, and instead of passing over my crouch, it hit the top of my head and glanced away. Whether that served as a stimulus, shaking me out of an idle doze, I couldn't say, but the next delivery was again short and I pulled it for six.

'I have only once been "pinned" square on, and that was at Luton in 1977. Our John Player League match against Northants had been reduced to a ten-

Joel Garner (5–38 in 11 overs) in the Prudential World Cup Final and (6–29 in 10.3 overs) in the Gillette Cup Final. The figures speak for themselves. His height and bounce make it awkward batting against him anywhere. Amongst other problems his hand tends to appear over most sightscreens, including the one at Lord's.

over slog by rain, and in such lottery circumstances you tend to allow more risks to creep into your batting. The shot I played against Alan Hodgson was typical of such situations, and the ball flew off the top edge into the bridge of my nose. It was the end of the game, as far as I was concerned. I crumpled up on the pitch and was subsequently ferried to hospital for two stitches. Both my eyes were closed, and I must have looked a fearful sight when I returned to the ground.

'Surprisingly perhaps, that injury kept me out of the game for only six days. The following Saturday, I was back in the side for a Championship match and, ironically, our opponents were against Northants and I walked out to bat to face the man who had put me in hospital. This time, however, conditions were very different. It was a dry wicket at Leicester, and there was no conceivable reason for the for the ball to fly. Despite all that, I was a little slow to get into position against anyone of any pace and possibly many others would have felt the same. I began to feel better once I had hit Hodgson through mid-on for four, and my confidence received the best possible convalescence when I went on to get a hundred the following day against Warwickshire.'

In the First Test against India at Edgbaston in 1979, Gower scored a double-century for the first time in his career. But he confesses he might have been out to any one of the first three balls he received. It was all down to his routine in the dressing-room before going out to bat.

'I'm not a good watcher. I don't always enjoy watching the play, particularly before batting, and in Australia on my first tour, there were many times when I saw very little of the day's play at all, either because I didn't want to or, on occasions, because I was "banned". Among the superstitions of the side is that, if things are going well on the field, you must change nothing in the dressing-room. So those who have not been watching are not allowed to come out during the middle of a partnership.

'In the Fifth Test at Adelaide, I didn't see one shot of the stand between "Chat" Taylor and "Dusty" Miller which virtually won the game for us. "Guy" Botham was banned and confined to the dressing-room with me, and when he lost patience and poked his head round the door for a peep at the action, "Dusty" was immediately out!

'At Edgbaston, I had a long wait to bat, following a good stand between Geoff Boycott and Graham Gooch, and I spent a lot of it watching the game on television. The picture was fuzzy at one point, so I got up to adjust the set. I was still fiddling with the monitor, no nearer to a clear picture, when I heard a shout from outside. I was in. I walked out blinking at the sunshine, having come straight from the relative darkness of the dressing-room, and if the first three balls had been ''jaffas'', I would probably have been walking back again.

'It is unusual for me to be that surprised by having to go in. Normally, if I'm batting at number five, I will have my box and thigh-pad on as soon as the first wicket falls, to avoid the batsman's nightmare of being next in and not having your gear on. But the adrenalin really starts pumping when the second wicket falls.

'That wicket brings a jerk of tension to me, drags me down to earth again if I've been relaxing and forces me to concentrate on the innings ahead. The pads go on, then the gloves – and if I am in swiftly, with a rapid loss of the third wicket, then it is generally not a bad thing for my personal game.

'I get easily bored when I'm waiting to go in. I will take my gloves off, then put them on again, fiddle with my bat and play a few shots in front of the mirror. Then I might sit down and try to relax,

Left Batting against Imran Khan, timed as one of the three fastest bowlers in the world in a competition in Perth, Western Australia, 1978–79. You may have spotted that the bat is facing the wrong way for this to be the completion of an orthodox pull shot. The ball is safely in Rod Marsh's hands behind the stumps having easily by-passed the bat, which I have dragged under the path of the ball having realised there was no chance of connecting with any profit.

Right Imran compelling evasive action at the Oval during the Courage Challenge 1979. Not the perfect way to duck, as I have taken the eyes off the ball, but at least I am well underneath the ball and even if it had not bounced as much, there is always the helmet to save serious injury – surely that cannot be a bad thing.

but if I put down my bat and gloves I always make a mental note of where they are. It avoids an embarrassing search!

'After 15 minutes or so, I am normally calm again, but when that third wicket does go, the real surge of nerves hits me like an electric shock stimulating the system.

'Most batsmen see the first ball as the important opening hurdle to negotiate, and I am no exception. There is a lot to learn from this first delivery. Depending on how good a ball it is, I can assess the pace of the pitch, the speed of the bowler, the light – and also how I am feeling.

'It is probably fair to say that I am a mood batsman, and if I swish at the first ball when I should have left it alone, it tells me that I must take a hold of myself and concentrate harder. Rather perversely, I often find that if I start badly, it is a good sign. I will improve steadily and work up to a peak. If I start well, feeling confident from the start, I often never reach that peak.

'The nerves are obviously biting hardest early in the innings, but it can be a mistake for me to make up my mind that I must defend for a while. I did so at Edgbaston in 1978, when I started my Test debut innings for England. The first ball, I had de-

Leaving the field after scoring 199–6 in the Courage Challenge Final 1979. Adrian Murrell's note on the photo reckoned I was dejected – actually I just felt exhausted. I did not feel dispirited – at least I had set some sort of total for Clive Lloyd to chase. Pity he made it.

cided, must just be played quietly. I must do nothing silly, just wait around for a while and have a look at things. So much for that resolution. It was a short ball and I hooked it for four.

'My first thought then was "What have I done now?" It was an extravagant, impulsive way to get off the mark for England, but it was not just a rush of blood to the head. It was a short, bad delivery – and that is the same whether its your first or five-hundredth ball.

'I don't worry too much about double figures but nor, at an early stage of an innings, do I concern myself with fifties and centuries. My next nervous target is 30. It is all too easy, once you have a dozen or so runs on the board, to relax. Complacency can creep into my game, and it has done on innumerable occasions, so I have deliberately set myself this rather unglamourous mark of 30, simply to keep my adrenalin pumping and retain my concentration.

'If I'm getting close to fifty, I have two conflicting thoughts. I want to tighten up again, to make sure I reach the magic figure, but I also feel the need to carry on playing my shots, which is the natural way for me to bat. Perhaps I am particularly vulnerable in that period, because I know I've been out many times between 46 and 56. But on the other hand, although I have not made many hundreds, I had never been out in the eighties or nineties until one day towards the end of July in 1979, when John Emburey got me out for 98.'

Schoolboys will always think of their heroes as unsmiling men with vast talents and never a hint of nerves. In most ways, David Gower fits the bill, because, with him, there are very few hints of nerves. But, believe me, they are there.

6. England

England v Pakistan 1978, First Test, Edgbaston and my Test debut. Left to right. Back row: Radley, Miller, Botham, Hendrick, Edmonds, Gower, Wood. Front row: Roope, Willis, Brearley, Old, Taylor.

David Gower made his England debut on June 1st 1978 and hooked his first delivery in Test cricket for four. With a similar lack of formality, he was to settle into the England side as if he had been there years.

Commenting on the sort of Test baptism which is dreamed up in heaven – Gower went on to score 58 and England beat Pakistan by an innings with a day to spare – pace bowler and vice-captain Bob Willis said: 'Some people are born to be Test cricketers. On this evidence, David Gower is one of the lucky few.'

Gower made his maiden England century in his Fourth Test and did not fail once in the six matches of the 1978 summer. He became a star, perhaps not overnight but certainly in the space of two run-filled months. By the end of the 1979 English season, Gower had played 16 Tests, scored more than 1,000 runs and was averaging 52. He was clearly to be a part of the England side for a considerable time to come, barring a dramatic loss of form, and playing for England, equally, had become a valued and important part of his life – at a far younger age than most England batsmen of this or any earlier generation.

He is one who enjoys studying people, their habits and personalities, and this chapter sets out his views on the men with whom he now spends a considerable part of his life . . . the England team.

GEOFF BOYCOTT: 'We are opposite in every way, yet despite that we seem to have a good relationship on the field. Geoff has been batting at the other end for much of the time during my two best Test innings – the century against Australia at Perth in December of 1978 and the double-century at

Above The Second Test at Lord's, 1979 and Mike Brearley makes a superb catch, low to his left hand to dismiss Sunil Gavaskar and give Ian Botham his 100th Test wicket. 'Both' shows his delight, on the left, with other fielders Bob Taylor, Phil Edmonds (background), Mike Hendrick, Mike Brearley (on floor) and Graham Gooch. The wicket followed three of four balls of softening up on 'Both's' part before the edge was eventually found – all in all a first class wicket. Opposite 'Keep playing youth.' 'And you, Fiery.' A break during the First Test against India at Edgbaston, 1979. Little pieces of encouragement like this have seen Geoffrey and myself through two notable partnerships, this one at Birmingham and one against Australia in the Second Test at Perth in December 1978.

Edgbaston in 1979 – and I believe his presence gives me a subconscious feeling of security. It is impossible to say that anyone simply will not get out, but at least I know Geoffrey will never give his wicket away lightly.

'He has often said to me "I wish I could bat like you" and I have never yet decided whether he is being sarcastic or serious. But I suppose it must be true that if you put together Geoff's temperament and technique and my willingness to play with freedom and fluency, the result could be formidable.

'One thing about Geoff can never be denied – he knows the game inside out. There are very few people I have met with his fund of cricketing knowledge, and although I do not go out of my way to pick his brain, he is always worth listening to when he has some advice.

'If his batting has a weakness it is the well-chronicled one of unpredictable running. If I am batting with him, my philosophy is to call every ball. Boycs does not mind being sent back as long as the shout is loud and good.

'Off the field, I see little of him, apart from when our paths happen to cross by travelling in the same car or meeting in a restaurant. We are, frankly, a generation apart and one could not expect our social lives to coincide. In the dressing-room, however, he seems to be a magnet for all the mickey-taking, and manages to reply with a fair bit of his own. Geoff and "Both" are constantly at each other – "Both" gave him the nickname "Thatch" for obvious reasons alluding to his hair – but a mutual respect for each other's talents underlies the sarcasm.'

IAN BOTHAM : 'Being original about "Guy the Gorilla" is not easy these days. So much has been spoken and written about him that even the distant cricket follower could be excused for believing he knew him as a friend. Most of the stories are true. He is brash, belligerent and highly competitive, and these virtues have been known to upset the weak at heart. His skills are emphasised by their dramatic unpredictability. In his batting and his bowling, he will never tire of trying something different. It can make him a difficult batting partner, but it certainly ensures he is a compelling cricketer. When he is bowling, he just loathes being taken off. He would bowl all day if he could, and there have been several notable occasions when he has almost done so – I think particularly of that marvellous final day of the 1979 Cornhill series against India when Mike Brearley just let him bowl and bowl for hours on end.

'Everyone knows he hits the ball a long way and loves bowling, of course, but I often think his fielding skills are underestimated. He looks casual in those close positions and has occasionally been caught with his hands on his knees, but he has also taken some memorable catches. Above all, he is brave. During the Australian tour of 1978–79, he was struck a sickening blow on the side of his helmet while fielding at short-leg. I was rooming with him at the time – and I am probably almost alone in knowing just how much it hurt him!

'He possesses endless energy, both on and off the field, and is the most boisterous member of the dressing-room, ever fond of the practical joke or

the loud story. I can only say that, on the few occasions when he has nothing better to do, he winds down with a marathon sleep.

'Guy is decisive about his likes and dislikes, in terms of people as well as material things and habits. If he does not like you, he won't hide it. He also has strong views on team topics – he is commercially aware but could never be ruled by cash because he puts such a high value on his sparetime interests. He loves to shoot, to play golf and watch football. He enjoys privacy so he will never seek too many public appearances. And, in that, I certainly sympathise with him.'

PHIL EDMONDS: 'Known as Maggie (christened when Mrs Thatcher was leader of the opposition), Goat (for unprintable reasons) or Henri (his middle name), Philip is a natural cricketer who will create any challenge for himself. It can be a great virtue or a failing. His batting, for instance, has enormous potential which, I am sure he would be first to admit, he has not always exploited. When I was at London University, I spent a day at Lord's watching Middlesex play Northants and saw Philip score a magnificent 93, hitting everything out of sight. Then, with his maiden century looming, his contrary nature seemed to demand that he should try to clear the one man on the boundary, at long-on. Predictably, he was caught there.

'When he is bowling, he loves the challenge of a good batsman against him, but he expects every ball to pitch on leg stump and turn to hit off. He hates fielders letting him down with drops or fumbles, but most of his retributions are thrown out to amuse himself. On or off the field, he enjoys casting down the bait for a row, testing out characters and reactions. He is a man who can seem over-

Phil Edmonds, the other half of the Middlesex 'spin twins' with John Emburey. 'Henri' enjoys experimenting with flight and even wrist spin at opportune moments, but has the ability to bowl as tightly as anyone under limited over conditions. Although he missed out on the 1979–80 Tour, I cannot believe he will not return to the fold at some stage.

bearing at first meeting, but I have grown to like him a lot.

'As a supremely confident and intelligent man, he has many advantages over most cricketers, but is acutely aware that life at the top is short and that it is important to make the most of it. As a room-mate, however, he was not my ideal, because his rising habits are in direct conflict with mine. He likes to be up by six o'clock. Not only that, but to immediately have the radio on (always a world news programme) and to throw open the curtains to devour the morning papers. He is also the only cricketer I know who takes the Financial Times into breakfast each morning.'

JOHN EMBUREY: 'A Middlesex team-mate of Phil Edmonds and, together, they form probably the best spin partnership in county cricket. "Embers", the off-spinner, had to wait a very long time for his chance at county level, then managed a dramatic elevation into the England side. Although he was not able to retain his place throughout 1979, I rate him as possibly the best off-break bowler in the country, because he varies his flight, length and pace so much.

'I have had a number of interesting duels with him when I've been batting, and have not always come through them. Embers knows his cricket and, like so many bowlers, loves his batting. He is rather a restricted batsman, but has played some very useful innings for country and county – and is always visibly disappointed when he fails.'

John Emburey has been described as the best English off-spin bowler and he certainly varies his flight and pace more cleverly than most. On a personal score, honours between John and myself are fairly even, though the last we met in a championship game I at least got 98 before driving him to long-off, a case of overambition on my part as much as deception on his. Here he is shown batting against Australia at Adelaide in January 1979, when his 42 runs were most welcome. Anyway, we have seen enough photographs of 'Ernie' bowling.

GRAHAM GOOCH: 'Despite a dour public image, he is one of the funniest characters in the dressing-room. His humour has probably emerged over more recent years to coincide with his development as a player. He lets himself go now, and combines a natural wit, helped by his rustic Essex accent, with a great sense of timing. His mimicking of Geoff Boycott's Yorkshire accent is hilarious, and I'm pleased that millions of people have now seen his impersonations of famous bowlers, which have progressed from his benefit match party piece to the Test match stage, to great effect.

"Zap," so named because of his Mexican-type moustache, is one of my particular friends in the side and I am as happy in his company as with anyone. He is living proof that cricket, even at the highest level, can and should be enjoyed, and he has the ability to see the funny side of things on the field and break up what might have been becoming a dull day. Although there is a natural disappointment that his first Test hundred had not arrived by the end of the 1979 summer, he hits the ball so powerfully and cleanly that it seemed to me it could only be a matter of waiting. He hits the spinners well, stands up to the quick men without any fears and plays his shots as I like to. In many ways, we are two of a kind.'

MIKE HENDRICK: 'Hendo may carry around an argicultural image, possibly exacerbated by the acquisition of his beard, and perhaps he likes to do nothing to discourage it. In fact, however, it is far from the truth. A blunt but intelligent man,

Graham Gooch in typically aggressive pose. Combining basic strength and heavy well-balanced bats, 'Zap' can hit the ball a long way, taking a particular delight in depositing spinners out of the ground. Very good to watch in that mood, especially from the non-striking end, though the pavilion is safer.

Mike Hendrick bowling against N.S.W. at Sydney, November 1978. Even Mike, whose pace is fast-medium rather than genuinely fast, has launched himself well off the ground after delivery. The non-striking batsman is Peter Toohey who did not perform during the Test matches as well as we originally feared he might, except for his 81 not

out in Perth. Tom Brooks is the Umpire, a very
likeable and honest character who eventually felt
obliged to withdraw from umpiring in Test Cricket
after the Perth Test Match of that Tour.
Incidentally the hill in the background looks fuller
then than during the Sixth Test Match –
Australians hate watching their side lose.

he appreciates a lot that is happening around him, but avoids involving himself in issues of politics and finance.

'A superb seam bowler who will sometimes move the ball too much off the wicket when conditions are in his favour, he is also a quiet, dry wit. He appreciates the humour of Monty Python and Kenny Everett, just as I do, and goes through a hilarious routine with Geoff Miller when they pretend to be Sam and Arthur, the flat-cap Derbyshire miners drinking in their local.

'Volatile on occasions, Hendo is generally a placid man whose outside interests include shooting, which he does with "Both" at every opportunity, and drinking good beer. After a game, however, he values privacy and will insist on drinking his pint in the company that he chooses.

'When we roomed together on the last three weeks of the 1978–79 tour, Hendo ordered hot chocolate in the room every night, for both of us. On one occasion, it took so long in arriving that Hendo was asleep, so I summoned "Bluey" Bairstow from across the corridor to have his share. A day or so later, we both fell asleep waiting . . . because we had ordered it for Bluey's room number in error, and the room waiter had woken him up with an unwanted drink.'

JOHN LEVER: 'Perhaps because they are both part of the infamous Essex humour, J. K. Lever has a very similar "lunatic" wit to Graham Gooch. He can see the fun in most situations, and is a tremendous asset in our dressing-room because he is generally so happy. It has been J.K.'s ill fortune to be twelfth man many more times than any other player in recent years, yet he has always managed to swallow his pride and get on with the duties – the most important of which is keeping everyone happy, in which he has no problems.

'There is a sane and analytical side to him when the occasion demands. He is a leading member of the Cricketers' Association, the nearest thing to a players' union, and in any discussions on the game he is appreciative of others' skills and equally quick on their weaknesses – which, for the 100-wickets a season bowler he has become, must be a great asset.

'Apart from the obvious left-arm variation which he gives any attack, his threat comes from variable

John Lever. Much has been said about 'J.K.' as a bowler and character. It is all true as he is not only a very fine swing bowler, but constantly entertaining off the field. One of the qualities that makes a player into a 'good tourist'. You can see his on-field determination evident in the photographs. For once 'J.K.' seems to be wearing orthodox bowling boots with the higher ankle supports, as mostly and unusually he bowls in less supportive cricket shoes.

swing. There are times when, batting against him, one can be lulled into the assurance that the ball is swinging very little, only to find the next one moving several feet, in either direction.

'Naturally, he has been unlucky to be left out of the side as often as he has – his only weakness against those who have played is that he is not as fast – but when he has been chosen, he has always relished being involved. Like any bowler with pride, he hates being what we know as the L.R.B. ... the last resort bowler.'

GEOFF MILLER: 'The first time I faced "Dusty", he pushed me onto the back foot and bowled me with his faster ball. In the second innings, keen for revenge, I swept him straight into the hands of deep square-leg. Since then, I have always looked forward to, and enjoyed, the challenge of batting against him. Some people criticise him for bowling his off-spin too fast and flat, but his answer is that he has always bowled that way – and, certainly, on his home wickets in Derbyshire, he will get people out by bowling that way. He is aware, however, that his bowling peak, to date, came in Australia in 1978–79 when he gave the ball a lot more air, bowled it slower and developed a loop in his flight.

'I think he is nervous about his batting, a lack of confidence which comes with the long wait for his maiden century. Although he is not a powerful player, he hooks and drives well and has played a number of invaluable innings for England. He is immensely serious when it comes to cricket, but has a wry humour at other times and is very easy to get on with. When I have roomed with him on tour, we have regularly been chided for being sleepy. Like me, he has the ability to doze off in planes and

Geoff Miller, during his most welcome 64 at Adelaide during the Fifth Test, January 1979. His main disappointment is never yet scoring a first class hundred, but on many occasions he has scored most useful fifties such as this one in support of Bob Taylor's 97. I hope he will not have to look back on his 98 not out against Pakistan for ever as the closest he had been to that century.

dressing-rooms, and dislikes getting up early in the morning.'

CHRIS OLD: '"Chilly" was the natural nickname for C. Old and it is also fitting because he does not like heat at all. He would have won the prize for the whitest body after four months on tour in Australia.

'He is a natural cricketer with plenty of innate talent, and even in my short time with the team, has had some memorable Test moments, notably his four wickets in five balls against Pakistan at Edgbaston in 1978. When he is bowling well and fully fit, he is a very difficult customer – a great, classical action to all those who do not have to face him.

'A very sociable and warm-hearted man, he provided the "in-room entertainment" with a cassette player when he was my first roomie on an England tour. He was also the first to congratulate me on my hundred in Perth and, another little thing that has always stuck in my mind, he predicted my double-century in 1979 by telling me that "one day soon, it will just happen".'

DEREK RANDALL: 'As a nervy, slightly self-conscious person, "Arkle" finds it difficult to get on with some people, but I like him a lot. His nervous energy rules his cricket. It is prominent in the field, where he is always doing something restless or unusual, and in his batting. He is moving well before the ball is released and seems to find it impossible to stand still between deliveries.

'For all that, he is a super player when in form, and has proved that he can play either as the aggressor or the defender. The contrast was brought home to me when I admired his 150 in ten hours which effectively won us the Fourth Test in Sydney in January, 1979, and then fielded against him four months later as he destroyed the Leicester-shire attack with a century before lunch for Notts, timing every shot almost to perfection.

'Arkle can be scatterbrained at times and has a reputation for leaving bath taps running. He is also not the tidiest of characters, but as a room-mate, he is quiet and concerned. He likes to keep in touch with his wife and he generally falls into the early-to-bed and early-to-rise category. Another one unlike me ...'

Batting with Derek Randall can be a matter of making sure nothing silly occurs. We all know he is very quick and so does he, so the temptation to steal inordinately quick singles is always present. At least I feel I have enough speed to avoid too much trouble but you have to make very sure that 'Arkle' does not attempt the impossible. In this innings he played very well – he was restrained and responsible – but, as if to prove what I have said, was eventually run out after a misunderstanding with Botham. For more comments on running with Derek see Geoff Boycott.

BOB TAYLOR: 'Once you have said that Bob Taylor is quiet, likeable, modest and superbly efficient as a wicketkeeper, it is all too easy to pass on. But that would be a trite dismissal of one of the nicest fellows I have met in cricket and certainly one of the finest, genuine wicketkeepers I have played with or against.

'His 'keeping may be unspectacular but it is unfailingly safe. The amount of bad sessions that Bob has had for England could be discounted as negligible, which is why I was riled by the Leeds crowd during the 1979 Test there. After one or two rare and unexpected slips by Bob, they began to chant "Taylor Out, Bairstow In". Support for their local man, you might call it. I called it unfair and unnecessary.

'The other great thing about Bob's wicketkeeping is that he keeps the rest of us on our toes. He

talks a good deal on the field, and always has a word for the bowlers. Often, I have seen him run 50 yards to clap Bob Willis on the back and give him a word of encouragement at the end of an over.

'His nickname, "Chat", has one of the better-known histories and it means just what it says. At parties and social occasions off the field, Bob is happy to talk to anyone, so long as his faithful pipe is within reach. At 38, he is no longer young for a wicketkeeper and his England chance came late, but he works so hard on his fitness that it does not seem to matter.'

PETER WILLEY: 'A Geordie of few words and blunt views, "Will" can be difficult to really get to know, but there is no doubt he has matured into a very fine all-round cricketer. Like Bob Willis, he has suffered knee injuries which could have forced

Bob Taylor during his 97 in Adelaide, Fifth Test 1979. Like Geoff Miller, he has not quite reached those magic three figures, but this 97 was a magnificent effort. Throughout his partnership with Geoff Miller, Ian Botham and I were forbidden by Bob Willis to watch any cricket for fear of breaking the spell. Unfortunately, the one time Ian looked out of the dressing room Geoff was out next ball.

him out of the game, yet he has fought back and made himself a better player. He is brave, not a bit ostentatious, and plays the game as he lives his life – simply but to effect.

'The quality of his batting is measured chiefly in his immense strength. During one John Player League game at Wellingborough – one of Northants' country grounds – I was fielding at extra-cover when he drove the ball at me so hard that my left hand, the only one I had time to get down, was numb for half-an-hour. And the ball travelled another 30 yards behind me!'

BOB WILLIS: 'I am told that "Goose" has quietened down somewhat since the start of his career, but he is still a very lively and unpredictable character. His dry humour and zany tastes still filter through occasionally, but in his senior position in the side he has devoted himself more to a role of leadership and example . . . and in that, he cannot be faulted.

'The injuries he came through would, I am sure, have forced most fast bowlers into a swift retirement. But Bob worked so hard on his fitness that he came back to bowl with as much life, and more control, than he had ever shown before. Every young fast bowler has a great deal to learn from him.

'Goose is very strong on team spirit, and worries over any little clashes. His judgements on players are strong and incisive – if he thinks anyone cannot bat, he will say so – and he is a man of moods over his own bowling. When things are going well – and on his day he can still destroy the best batting in the world – he is visibly motivated. If he is having a bad time he can become moody, and it is then that the spirit of the side which he has helped to nurture plays a great part.'

Bob Willis bowls Alan Border on the last morning of the Fifth Test in Adelaide, January 1979. Bob had not been at his penetrating best during the middle of the tour, but came back into form very nicely that morning taking three middle order wickets in quick succession.

7. A Day in the Life of a Test Player

The idea seemed foolproof. We were to select a day, at random, from the 1979 home Cornhill series against India, and chart David Gower's thoughts and movements, minute by minute and hour by hour. An illustration of the routine of a Test cricketer, in fact. For no particular reason, we chose the opening day of the Third Test, at Headingley, on August 16. For two particular reasons, it did not turn out quite as expected – Gower made the first nought of his Test career and less than three hours' play was possible before the Yorkshire weather turned sour.

While it was no longer an example of an idyllic day with England, however, these setbacks gave a better insight into the minds and personalities of the England players, and Gower in particular, as they coped with the two things every cricketer dreads. Failure and boredom ... The tedium of a rainy day, or even worse, of several successive wet ones, can be the biggest drag in a cricketer's existence. Having to handle a personal failure at the same time can breed despair. Sometimes, I am sure, a cricketer in such a situation wants the game to go away for ever. Gower naturally knew he would one day make a Test duck, but it did not make the moment any easier. The weather matched his mood, briefly at least.

The day, indeed, had started as it meant to continue. Gower, rising more leisurely than most on the first morning of a Test, had discovered that one of his ordered papers had not been delivered, and had then eaten a bad breakfast ...

'I always need an alarm call, even during Tests. Some of the side, particularly Bob Willis, find it very hard to sleep at all on the eve of an England match, but that is no problem to me. The phone rang at 8.30 am, and I felt relaxed enough to doze on for another 20 minutes before stirring myself into something near alertness.

'On tour, everyone except captain and vice-captain has to share, two to a room, but for home Tests, we all have separate rooms. In Leeds, as in most modern hotels, the comfort was functional rather than luxurious. A large double bed, colour television and telephone in the room, and a compact bathroom – all I need, anyway, for the room is to me little more than a place to put my head down.

'As usual, I had ordered three newspapers – the *Daily Telegraph*, the *Mail* and the *Star*. A scale from heavy to light reading, to suit all moods. I like to browse through them early in the morning, and keep them with me to read more thoroughly at slack times later in the day. Today, I was one short – the *Star* was missing and I felt oddly irritated by it.

'Most players like to surface for breakfast in the restaurant, and I am no exception. I find that meals served in the room are generally cold and verging on the inedible. It was 9.15 by the time I had washed, dressed, completed the morning constitutionals and negotiated the lift to the breakfast room, and by that time most of the lads had eaten and dispersed.

'Ian Botham and Dusty Miller were still there, so I joined their table and ordered fried eggs – my normal hotel breakfast menu, because I don't trust many places to do scrambled eggs the way I like them. This time, however, it was a bad decision. Both the eggs were hard instead of runny. Slightly dissatisfied, I finished the meal alone with two cups of tea, then collected my kit and joined Dusty, who

was waiting by his car in the hotel's own indoor private car park, to drive me to the ground. It makes sense in every way if we share cars for the daily hotel–ground trip; the harassed officials are pleased to have more parking space, and the Energy Secretary, I am sure, would be delighted with our efforts to conserve fuel.

'We were among the last to arrive in the dressing-room, which is not an unusual occurrence for me. It is not that I dislike getting there early – it has nothing to do with nerves or superstitions – it is simply that I seldom manage it. But it was still only a quarter to ten, which left ample time for all the pre-match jobs before the 11.30 start.

'The first task for almost all of us is always to organise complimentary tickets to be left at the gate for relatives or friends. We are allowed four per day each these days, which must make things a lot easier than when the restriction was two, but a lot of bartering still invariably goes on every morning, with players who need tickets for one day swapping with those who want them for another. Today, my priority was a ticket for my mother, who was driving up from Loughborough to watch. With that done, I returned to the dressing-room. I stopped to sign a couple of autographs, but if you linger outside, you could be trapped there all day. I never like to hang around for long at this stage.

'Having changed into my kit, I went into the outfield with Dusty for a short, loosening practice with

At Lord's in the Second Test, 1979 the Indian bowlers ruled the early part of the England innings as under heavy skies the ball swung and seamed appreciably. Derek Randall and I survived until the rain came, not without some luck, and were able to resume the day after under more favourable conditions. The ball did beat the bat however, as on this occasion from Dev when the ball bounced higher than usual from short of a length – could it have hit the ridge that we are told has been removed? Dev and 'keeper Reddy are both in pain while the slip is denying any responsibility for events. My thinking is to ignore that ball and carry on playing each ball as it comes.

bat and ball. The nets were erected in front of the pavilion, actually on the playing area – the muddy patches caused were to create problems when the rain arrived later – but I am something of a rarity about this sort of thing and seldom want more than a few balls thrown at me before the match begins. Others, notably Geoff Boycott of course, will invariably have a pretty long bat in the net.

'I found it noticeable at this stage that the lads were generally pretty relaxed, far less tension showing than there had been on the morning of a Test in Australia, for instance. There were exceptions: Bob "Goose" Willis is a nervous sort, anyway, and as he had missed the previous Test at Lord's with an injury, he was obviously a bit tense. Ian Botham too, although it surprises many people, is very nervous at this stage. In the dressing-room, he smokes incessantly before a match. But otherwise, perhaps because it was India we were playing and we had the subconscious feeling that we were better than them anyway, there were few visible signs of tattered nerve-ends.

'It is a religion now with most of us to do our routine of stretching exercises with our physio, Bernard Thomas, about an hour before the start. The fast bowlers never miss, and I like to be in on them because they really do get the stiffness out of my body and make me feel better tuned for the game. Some of the exercises bring a few laughs and titters from the crowd, but that no longer concerns us.

'"Both" was batting in the nets at the time, and we were midway through one of the stretches when he unwound an almighty drive which just cleared the captain's head and landed in the middle of our group, as if he was playing target golf. "Guy", of course, was hugely amused!

'As we were leaving the field, someone in the crowd yelled at me: "I want a hundred from you, today." My reply was something banal, such as "I wouldn't complain," but I was to remember that call rather grimly later.

'A few more autograph books were thrust my way as I reached the foot of the staircase which leads up to the dressing-rooms at Leeds, and I dutifully signed them before joining the usual chatter of the lads in the uncertainty of the wait for the toss. Mike Brearley, like me, had enjoyed a brief conversation of sorts with a spectator. He related to us that some fellow had told him he must be sure to win the toss. "Why?" Mike had inquired. "So I can watch Geoffrey Boycott bat, of course," had been the answer, apparently in a tone which suggested disbelief that anyone should come to a Test to see anything else ...

'While we were waiting, I summoned the boy who acts as slave and valet to us in the Headingley dressing-room and revels in the nickname of "Joe Ninety" – one of Willis's inspirations. I sent him to get some whitener for my pads and boots, and filled in time trying to smarten them up with a useless liquid which was far too thin for the job.

'As Scagg – Mike's nickname amongst the England lads – finally went out to the middle, "Henri" Edmonds became the topic of our attention. He was complaining that he rarely gets any lbw decisions when he is bowling, and we attempted to convince him that his appealing often sounds like sarcasm directed at the umpire. He was not convinced, of course.

'We were batting. The announcement from the captain brought my first flutter of nerves today. I immediately checked my kit to make sure everything was in its proper place and that I had not forgotten some vital piece of equipment. Then, as I was down to bat at four, I put on my box and thigh-pad, leaving only pads and gloves for the fall of the first wicket.

'Scagg and Geoff were both quiet before going out, as they always are. Wrapped up in thoughts of the innings ahead, few batsmen say much in the minutes before their innings.

'When the game was underway, the rest of us started a discussion on the winter tour of Australia ahead of us, chiefly in a commercial sense. Goose, Henri and Bob Taylor fired the conversation, and Bernie "The Bolt" Thomas was also involved as the man who does so much organisational work on tours.

'The debate rather lost its way when we touched on the subject of track suits. Henri, living up to his image as leader of the opposition, complained that the last set we were given had been semi-impermeable, and "Arkle" Randall, joining in for the first time, said in a mock-puzzled voice: "I thought that was something you did to your hair."

'Boycs getting out came as something of a stunner. The openers had been jogging on very well, passed fifty and looked in no trouble. Then Geof-

frey looked to hit Kapil Dev square on the off-side and was caught at gully. He came back slightly unsure of what had gone wrong and eager, as always, for other people's opinions. His own version was that the bat had twisted in his hand on making contact and, from where I sat, that looked the logical conclusion.

'This was the time for the butterflies to start work. I put on my pads, picked up my gloves and started on a piece of chewing gum, as I always do at this stage. I don't really like the stuff, but I find it settles me to chew for a while, and stops me getting dry in the mouth. By the time I go in, the gum is usually reduced to pulp and pretty tasteless.

'Goochy was out quickly, and the usual jolt to my system hit me with the awareness that I was in rather earlier than I had expected. Like a number of other players I know, I felt more relaxed as soon as I set foot on the pitch, concentrating my mind on getting over the obstacle of the first ball.

'As it turned out, that was no problem, but in the next over Scagg was out to Ghavri and I knew then that my priority must be to carry on playing, to stay in and ignore risks, because someone needed to play a long innings.

'It was not going to be me. I allowed one or two deliveries to pass through, then blocked one from Kapil in the middle of the bat and instantly felt a bit more confidence seep into my mind. It was short-lived. The next ball swung into me late as I went across to it defensively, and I had no complaints about being given out leg-before.

'Dad – I think I got it wrong.' The Second Test at Lord's 1979 and Ghavri has bowled from very wide on the crease and angled the ball into the stumps past my front pad. Quite why I should err like this, in full flow, remains a mystery – just put it down to 'batsman's error'. When I got back to the dressing room, and before anyone else said it, I mentioned that it was ironic that I, having played so many shots that day, should get out not offering one at all! As you can see by the relatively upright position of the off-stump, the ball only just made contact.

'What were my first thoughts? Certainly, that this was my first duck in Test cricket. It had to come some time, but it is still a depressing feeling when it does. I also felt, rather obscurely, that the wheel of fortune had turned on me, because I recalled in that moment how close I must have been to being lbw first ball in the Second Test at Lord's. I escaped that time, and went on to make runs. Justice caught up, I suppose.

'The usual bad-lucks greeted me in the dressing-room, but everyone is wise and tactful enough to talk very little to a man who is just out. No-one is at their chummiest in the few minutes that follow. I watched the fateful ball again on the television action replay and was pleased to note that it seemed a better delivery than I had thought at the time.

'We were four down for not very many and in the sort of trouble that none of us could have envisaged. In the space of half-an-hour, the atmosphere in the dressing-room had changed from chirpy confidence to quiet, subdued anxiety, and I was glad when lunchtime followed swiftly and we were able to get out and breathe for a while.

'There was nothing too solemn about the meal, though, and when play restarted, Goochy and I stayed down in the dining-room with J. K. Lever, the unlucky one to be made twelfth man ... again. I produced my camera and took one or two pictures of the other two clowning with some food, and after twenty minutes, we trooped back into the dressing-room.

'Despite one or two alarms, Arkle and Guy were still in when the rain started just before three. It set in so quickly that it was soon obvious we would not play again today, and we were left – at 88 for four still in something of a predicament – with time to kill before the umpires formally called it off.

'Guy was loud and boisterous as ever, Henri had his usual amount to say, and the Essex boys, J.K. and Goochy, were bubbling amusingly, but after the first half-hour, boredom inevitably began to set in.

'A row broke out when BBC decided to re-run the highlights of the 1975 World Cup to keep their viewers relatively happy. Some of us were interested, but others wanted it switched off. Bob Willis was the prime mover against watching because, he said, he had no wish to watch Gary Gilmour bowl us out again!

'The endless stream of bats and books to autograph came round, together with a few glossy magazines of dubious taste. I read the newspapers again for something to do and eventually, after tea, Peter West came on the box and said they were going to show some of the high and low spots of what play we had managed. Almost everyone was interested now, but there was an exception. Arkle had survived a loud appeal for lbw while he was batting, and as it came up on the screen, he suddenly started singing, banging his boots together and generally making a dreadful noise, with his back turned to the television. Not only was he determined not to see how close he was to being out, he also didn't want to hear the commentator's verdict.

'Soon after five, Dickie Bird came into the dressing-room and apologetically relieved us all by telling us it was over for the day. Some of the lads stayed on for a drink in the sponsors' tent – a tradition at Tests, these days – but I went back to the hotel and spent an hour reading a magazine in my room. Then, after a shower to liven myself up, I joined Bernard Thomas, Bob Taylor, Alec Bedser and Ken Barrington for a drive to Brian Close's house, in Bernard's spacious Rolls-Royce.

'Closey was throwing a party for the players, selectors and various other people, but our first problem was finding his house, which is stuck on top of a hill up a dirt track. With that done, I settled down to enjoy an evening with rather less restraint than I would have shown if I might have been batting the following morning.

'J.K., Guy and Goochy joined us, with Lever wearing Guy's cloth cap. Within half-an-hour, none of us were bare-headed. Closey's cloakroom had been raided and we came up with two riding hats, a camouflage floppy for Guy and something Goochy claimed which made him look like a Polish train conductor.

'We supped beer from some of Closey's many prize tankards and tucked into the generous buffet. We did our socialising bit for the sake of diplomacy and public relations, then, when the selectors had departed, had a session in the kitchen which I can excuse as sorrow-drowning. We left at about eleven, hurried through the teeming rain to our cars and drove back into the city and to the hotel. It had been a bad day. No runs

*Courage Challenge Final 1979. How to keep your
left toe in the crease despite losing balance.
Actually Rod Marsh seems to have lost interest
even if I were to slide out of my ground at this
stage.*

for myself, the team in trouble and the weather
appalling. But if things can go as badly as that, and
we could still come out of it enjoying an evening
as we did tonight, the spirit in this side can't be bad.
With that thought, I went off into my usual deep
sleep, not to be disturbed until the telephone wakes
me again at 8.30.'

200 Not Out

Above Batting during my highest ever 200 not out against India at Edgbaston – not surprisingly my happiest memory of the 1979 season. I took a new bat out with me at the start of the innings to try and change my luck. Say no more! Here it seems to be in control just guiding the ball down behind point: could be two runs if we push it.

Opposite What I like about this pull shot is that it is more controlled than usual and the ball even looks to have gone down. A week before the Test I had played against the Indians at Leicester on a bouncy wicket and pulling had been risky.

short ball arriving at different heights and paces. At Edgbaston the pitch was slower and flatter and the pull or hook was definitely 'on' against Ghavri and Dev, with some short balls only getting up about waist height, as it looks to have done in this shot.

200 Not Out

More runs in my 200 – in one of my favourite areas – just behind square on the off-side, this time off the spinner. There are times when I try to guide the ball into this area off deliveries not really short enough and also alarmingly straight, but I have at least avoided getting out like that recently. The wicketkeeper is Reddy, whose agility did not match that of Kirmani, the man whom he replaced in the Indian Test side and who in fact regained his place as soon as the Indians got home. The slip is Viswanath.

*I always appreciate a glass of water, more
refreshing than orange juice or anything else –
they don't serve ale on the field. The Indians still
seem happy enough, their 12th and 13th men are
Yajurvindra Singh who played at the Oval and
Patel who did not play in the series.*

200 Not Out

I have just pushed one to mid-off off Venkat to reach 50 and am in the process of telling myself to keep going and not do anything silly – aiming now for 100. The same thought processes need to be completed at each landmark – the obvious ones being 50, 100 and so on, but in my case I like to get past 30 initially and then the next ten runs after each landmark during which one can relax and so give one's wicket away, for example between 50 and 60, or 100 and 110. Applauding is Venkat and behind me is Kapil Dev, India's only wicket taker in this innings with five wickets for 146.

Aftermath of success – five minutes with the
Press. 'How did you feel?' 'Over the moon, guv!'
Happily my imagination runs to more than that.
Note the glass of water – unadulterated. There is
plenty of time for more serious relaxation later,
although that night was spent at Walsall Golf
Club over dinner with the editorial board of
Wisden Cricket Monthly.

8. Touring

At the tender age of five, David Gower was chased by an elephant and then confronted by a herd of buffalo on the game reserves of East Africa. Good practice, perhaps, for the trials against Hogg, Roberts, Thomson and company ahead of him. If these early tests of bravery were not passed with raw, young courage – he justifiably panicked on both occasions – they at least failed to turn him against travelling. Numerous foreign trips later, he still looks forward to each one and, for an international cricketer, is fortunate to be blessed with the phlegmatic personality which never frets over being away from home for lengthy periods.

It might, of course, be very different if and when he becomes a married man, for it is then that a sizeable extra strain is placed on every top-class professional cricketer. A bachelor without serious ties can happily take every opportunity of touring abroad and relish each day of it with scarcely a care for home; a man with a wife and children, a house and a mortgage, has different pressures.

Gower's love of travel was no doubt fostered by

On parade at Melbourne during the Sir Robert Menzies Memorial Match against Victoria (1978). These official tour blazers, nicknamed 'Admiral's Gear' because of all the braid, were worn only at cricket grounds for photos and other prestigious events. Elsewhere the less ostentatious light blue blazers were worn. Still, they were my first tour blazers and I was proud enough to wear them, whatever my preferences for casual clothing.

growing up in sunny climes of his father's colonial service postings. Much of his first five years was spent in Tanganyika, as it was then called, but his memories are understandably restricted largely to the final months ... the game reserves and the wild beasts which looked even more awesome to one of his short years and stature.

'We were driving a land-rover through one of the game parks one day, with an elephant lumbering after us. I was not too concerned, as I recall, until the land-rover stalled and the elephant closed in on us ...

'The driver got the vehicle going again and we escaped down the road, only to meet a herd of buffalo. They were still about a quarter of a mile ahead, but that was close enough for me. In my wild panic, I decided I had seen enough, opened the side door and began to climb out of the land-rover. I was pulled back in, and as I slammed the door shut, the noise was enough to scatter the entire herd, which, when I had time to calm down, made me feel rather proud of my five-year-old self.

'I remember little of the rest of my time in Tanganyika, apart from the endless days on the beach ... and my first attempt to drive a car. My parents were lazing on the beach when I slipped away to our Ford Anglia, clambered into the driver's seat and turned the key. The car, still engaged in gear, leaped forward about a yard and little D.G. was panicking again!'

At 13, Gower went on a ski-ing holiday in Switzerland with his family and again exercised his penchant for finding danger. Apart from the more customary tumbles on skis, he managed to fall off a ski-lift which was winching him up the mountainside.

Touring Party 1978–79. My first international Tour and associated with happy memories, not least winning 5–1 in Australia. Left to right. Back row: Randall, Radley, Lever, Miller, Botham, Edmonds, Hendrick, Emburey, Gooch, Gower, Tolchard, Saulez (Scorer). Front row: Thomas, Boycott, Willis, Brearley, Insole (Manager), Taylor, Old, Barrington (Assistant Manager).

His cricket travelling began late in 1974 when, at the age of 17, he was chosen for a representative side calling themselves The Crocodiles and comprising outstanding cricketers from eight English public schools. The tour was of slightly less than a month and the organisers were St Andrews College in Grahamstown, near the South African city of Port Elizabeth. St Andrews had made their own tour of English schools, including Gower's King's, and this was to be the reciprocal trip. Chris Cowdrey was The Crocodiles' captain, starting a long-standing relationship with Gower as cricketers and friends, and Gower, for the first time, spent Christ-

mas away from home, on a beach thousands of miles from England.

Apart from a one-week trip to Holland, notable only because he was given a new bat as Batsman of the Week – and lost it within a fortnight – his next foreign assignment was to the West Indies as a member of the successful England Young Cricketers party of 1976. The team was peppered with names which have since found prominence at county, if not England level, including Mike Gatting and Ian Gould of Middlesex, Cowdrey and Paul Downton of Kent, Richard Williams of Northants ...

'The tour took place in the middle of the English summer, but I went on it in good heart after scoring my maiden county century in my final innings in England. My form on tour was consistent and the cricket was generally good, but it is fair to say that my memories of the Caribbean are of the places, the people and the fun, rather than the games themselves.

'We played several matches in Barbados, and every night at the end of play, we would pile on the back of mini vans and race back to our hotel, which was positioned on Accra Beach. After a cool dip in the water, we played beach cricket, some-

Time to relax after a net at the Church of England School, Brisbane, before the First Test in 1978. John Lever is the man taking a quick breath before going under again while Mike Hendrick lurks with intent behind. I always appreciated the chance to relax by the pool if possible, thereby achieving the tan I needed to prove I had really been in the sun for four months.

times with the locals, until the light made it completely impossible. I also developed a passion for snorkelling, off Antigua, and I would sometimes go out for hours at a time. I have since also taken a liking to performing on top of the water with water skis.

'That winter, I went on my first trip with Derrick Robins, that rather controversial figure who has nevertheless done much to aid the development of English players and of the game itself in various parts of the world. This was a three-week stop in Canada, which ran into problems in Edmonton, where the anti-apartheid demonstrators picked on us as their practice targets for the Commonwealth Games two years later.

'DHR (Derrick's initials and common nickname) was criticised there as being a pawn of apartheid, because he lived in South Africa, but the demonstrators, as usual, had got their facts wrong. They were overlooking the fact that by organising teams to undertake multi-racial cricket tours out there, he had made considerable efforts to break down apartheid policies. At one stage on the trip, DHR was so upset by the harassment, and probably the personal slight against him, that he threatened to cancel all the remaining cricket, visit the scheduled places and simply play golf instead!

'I found Derrick a genial, but moody man, but there is no doubt his tours are well organised, and I was invited again the following year – an unforgettable trip to the Far East which gave me my first sight of exotic places like Colombo, Penang, Hong Kong and Singapore. The cricket, naturally enough, was not of any great standard, but there were some marvellous times off the field.

'In Kuala Lumpur, I stayed with a chap named Ronnie Quay, and I am sure he would not flinch if I called him a whizzkid playboy and the worst driver I have ever seen. One night, after a reception at the High Commission, he was driving us on to a party at the K.L. cricket club, when he scraped the car down the side of a lorry without appearing to notice or care. Later that same evening, he brought the car out of an alleyway at breakneck speed and scraped the other side of it down a wall. I was grateful to get my feet back on safe land.'

By the end of the 1977 home season, Gower had progressed rapidly enough to be considered an outsider for England's tour of Pakistan and New Zea-

land. He was overlooked to the benefit of his friend Gatting, but believes on reflection that he gained more value from a winter spent in Perth, playing grade cricket for Claremont-Cottesloe.

'I have never been to Pakistan and, from all the stories brought back by the other England lads, I am not all that sorry. Life in Perth was good. I spent five days a week on the beach, coached on certain evenings, and played for the club every weekend. The Packer players were banned from playing grade cricket that winter, but the standard was still highly competitive and I am sure I learned a good deal about the game during my stay. Certainly, it was ideal grounding for the following winter, and my first England tour.

'I cannot say it was a surprise to be selected in the squad for the Australia trip of 1977–78, as I had played in all the home Tests that summer and fared well. Neither can I recall exactly how I was told about my selection, but I have a feeling I heard it first on the radio on the day that the side was announced. Despite all that, it was a great relief, and gratifying to receive confirmation that the selectors had some faith in me for what was to be a momentous trip.

'After all the preliminaries of any trip, it is always good to get on the plane and get airborne. I think so, anyway, as I hate hanging around airports, I have no fear of flying and I can generally sleep very easily on any long flights. But there are others who think very differently. John Lever, for instance, hates flying and makes it noisily obvious. He will sit, strapped in his seatbelt and clutching the arms of his chair, chattering incessantly as the plane taxies for a take-off position. A few more in the side show their fear by the opposite reaction, becoming unnaturally quiet as take-off time approaches.

'The second early hazard on a tour is acclimatising, and recovering from the inevitable jet-lag. Again, I appear to be among the luckier ones. Whether or not this stems from my upbringing in a hot country I cannot say, but I love the sun and have never minded the physical feeling of being very hot. Bob Willis and Chris Old are two I have toured with who do not relish the heat and tend to avoid sun-tans as some would avoid cold showers.

'Chris, or "Chilly" as everyone calls him, was in fact my first room-mate, and immediately scored points with me because he had brought a portable tape player. Music is a great companion on tour, and a good deal of swapping of cassettes goes on throughout the trip.

'The idea, I presume, was that Chilly, as an experienced campaigner of five previous tours, would look after the new boy of the party, and he was certainly a valuable ally in the early weeks, which I spent chiefly finding my way and discovering the routines of a full England trip.

'For the first week, every day was much the same. We met outside the hotel in Adelaide at about 9.30 each morning, so I needed to force myself out of bed and eat some breakfast before that hour. Our cars – we had a fleet of sponsored vehicles in most cities – took us to the ground, where our training began with four or five laps of The Oval. At that hour of the day, and with the jet-lag still biting, it seemed a very big ground.

'After our stretching exercises with Bernie Thomas, we then had nets each side of lunch, finished for the day at about three o'clock and went back to the hotel for a lazy hour by the swimming-pool. It was a gentle routine, necessarily so for that stage of acclimatisation, because for four or five days nobody felt quite right.

'My introduction to top Australian cricket was traumatic, to say the least. Our opening match was against South Australia, and I was required to go into bat just as Clive Radley was being carried off to hospital. Rad had been hit on the head by a lifting ball from Rodney Hogg and had fallen back onto his stumps to cause his dismissal amid his pain.

'It is no use pretending that I was not apprehensive about it. I took guard over a patch of blood, fresh on the green of the pitch, and knew I was facing the bowler who was tipped to be the next in Australia's long line of pace bowlers. I had watched Hoggy bowl against Western Australia when I was in Perth a year earlier, but now he looked quicker, certainly more aggressive in his approach.

'I played and missed about four times, then ducked into a short one and took the ball behind the shoulder. It could have been a great deal worse, and after hitting a four I was on my way. I made 73 in the first innings, 50 in the second and came out of a shock defeat quite happy with my personal form. But within a few weeks, I was in a run-famine.

Opposite and overleaf A sequence showing the first Test dismissal of the Australian Tour 1978–79. Graham Wood (a left-hander) has pushed the ball gently to me at cover and called Gary Cosier for the run. This was very early on in the first morning of the game at Brisbane and all of us were keyed up and hoping for the breakthrough – I was very happy to oblige by running in and picking up the ball and throwing down the stumps underarm. Gary was only just out, as subsequent photographs proved and as can be seen by the way he has turned in the second photograph and is heading back to the crease. However, by the end of the sequence, he is heading towards the pavilion and Bob Willis, who was just out of the picture and looking very uninterested at the start, has managed a grin on his way to join the congratulations. The dismissal began a dismal morning for the Aussies who went into lunch 26 for 6. One point to note is Bob Taylor's footwear, a new sole comprising square rubber protrusions, a cross between a flat sole and spikes, in Bob's opinion very comfortable and giving him adequate grip on dry Australian surfaces. Some of our batsmen also swore by them, though I still preferred to have spikes in at least the front half of the boot while batting and on the heel as well for fielding.

83

Several more batsmen had been hit on the head and Bob Willis had "pinned" two in one match against Queensland just before the First Test. I was anxious, I confess. Short of runs and confidence, I had been called before the captain and manager for a chat. I wore a helmet in the First Test and psychologically felt more assured against the threat of Hogg.'

It hardly needs words from Gower to emphasise how well the rest of that series went for the England team. The 5–1 victory margin says all that and more. But for me, and for many others, the highlights of it all came shortly before Christmas at Perth when Gower, the tour baby, joined the senior pro Geoff Boycott in a crisis, proceeded to retrieve the innings and ultimately win the Second Test with a century as courageous and majestic as any one is likely to see from a young England batsman.

'One innings can rarely be compared properly with any other, but I do not mind saying that that was my most memorable innings so far, chiefly because of the way I made the runs but partly through the situation we were in when I went out to bat and also partly because it was at Perth.

'After the previous winter, it almost felt like going home again. I am not the sort of person who makes hundreds of friends and can't wait to see them all, but there were some genuinely nice people I looked forward to meeting again. I like the city, too, and from that innings on, I have a lot of time for the ground!

'Hoggy was bowling the third over of the game when he dismissed Graham Gooch and Derek Randall in the space of three balls. The captain saw us past lunch with "Boycs", but was out at 41, and I had to go in with Hoggy back for a fresh spell and firing very impressively.

'In my first over at the crease, he brought one up sharply and hit me on the fleshy part of the neck under the helmet. My instant impression was that I should feel hurt, but I didn't, and that instead of cringing and complaining I should simply try to show him that he had not hurt me. I got one off the edge past third slip to set me on my way, Hoggy was taken off again after one more over, and from then on I felt comfortable.

'Boycs and I were together out there for the best part of a playing day, and he seemed amused that I should go on batting the way I always have, waft-ing at and missing the odd wide one, while he ground out every run in his usual technical fashion. He smiled at me every now and again from the other end, and when we met in mid-wicket, he addressed me as "Young star". In replying, of course, I called him "Old star".

'I had reached my hundred just a few minutes before the end of the first day, and celebrated suitably that night. The next morning, I played myself in again, began to feel good, but then got the unplayable ball from Hoggy after making only one more run in half-an-hour.'

The stand between Gower and Boycott was fascinating for its contrasting techniques . . . as different as their two lifestyles. It would always be difficult to call Gower dedicated in the sense that Boycott is – but that should not be seen as a slight. Blessed with more natural ability, and the personality of a socialite, he lives a full life which is never dominated by the thought of an innings or a match. He admits, for instance, that he went out in Brisbane, with another England player, on the night before the First Test. He needed to, he says, to relax. 'We were both a little wound up, and thought that a social, but reasonable night out would be far more soothing than lying sleeplessly on a hotel bed for too many hours.'

He makes no secret of the fact that Australia's social scene was immensely appealing to him. 'The

Batting during my 102 during the Second Test at Perth 1978 and on the front foot, if not a long way. Most of the time against quick or even medium-pace bowling I would try to wait on the back foot for the ball, rather than commit myself onto the front – not advisable against fast, short-pitched bowling. Despite Perth being the warmest of the state capitals, normally it was not hot enough on the first day to stop me wearing a sleeveless sweater – some sort of superstition for me, if not an infallible one. The helmet I had worn for the first time at Brisbane in the previous test and found to be unobtrusive, if a little warm but a useful psychological comfort. To date I have not been struck on it.

great difference between there and England,' he says, 'is that if you feel like having a party in Australia, you can have it outside with very few weather worries.'

Like most of us, he was puzzled, not to say amused, by the Australians' habits of males ignoring their female partners on a night out. 'At any party or in any pub, the men all stand around at the bar with their drinks and the women are parked together in the corner with theirs. And that is where they stay until their man wants to go, which is normally not until he has had plenty to drink.'

'My memories of Melbourne are dominated by the amount of sport there was to see there. Even while we were staying, there was a major golf tournament, the Australian Open tennis and the famous Melbourne Cup horse-race, in which I won 20 dollars for a place in our sweepstake. It almost goes without saying that golden boy Ian Botham won the first prize.

'Sydney is probably my favourite city. The views, the beaches and the restaurants are all memorable, and we happened to be staying on the fringes of Kings Cross, which is Australia's equivalent of London's Soho. One night, one of the lads and I sneaked inquisitively into one of their grubby shops – the sort where you put 10 cents in the slot and get a dirty picture on a machine – and spent about five minutes there. As we were slipping out, glad that no-one had recognised us, some fellow sidled up and said: "Good luck tomorrow, lads".'

Gower is not one of those to suffer homesickness, or endure boredom on tour. Even at Christmas,

Here we are forcing off the back foot at the Second Test, Perth 1978. The ball seems to have ended up in front of square and it was probably not as hard as I intended. It looks as if I might have been sweeping the legspinner – judging from the dirt on my left pad. That was one of my more effective methods of scoring against Jim Higgs, made slightly less risky as I would have been hitting with the spin, except for occasions when I failed to read the googly.

Celebrations as we go two up after Perth.
Champagne must have been on hand, but at this
stage 'Both', 'J.K.', 'Dusty' and 'Hendo' are all on
Swan Lager – I cannot imagine where mine was.
The teddy was the property of two of our staunch
supporters who followed us around throughout the
series. The nonplayers Old, Edmonds (making
sure the bat is signed), Tolchard and Bernie
Thomas remain inside, while the quorum of
players pose for the cameras (left to right myself,
Botham, Boycott, Emburey, Taylor, Hendrick and
seated, Lever and Miller).

Christmas in Melbourne, 1978 and for the fancy dress luncheon originality went out of the window despite 45 minutes browsing in the costume department of the Festival Theatre, Adelaide (our previous stop before flying to Melbourne on Christmas Eve). Here the Chicago Pizza Pie Kid acknowledges an unknown heckler, water pistol temporarily out of sight.

when both ills afflict many players, he was happily active, first behind the bar as the players gave the traditional Christmas morning party to the press contingent, then in his cowboy outfit at the team's fancy dress lunch, and finally with friends for a convivial afternoon and evening.

'There were a number of unhappy players at Christmas, mainly the guys with children at home, of course. I was rooming with Arkle (Derek Randall) and he missed his wife and baby very badly. Bob Taylor and Chris Old were just the same, and it is at times such as these when the spirit of the side is really needed to give a lift to those who are moping.

'The system of two players to a room on tour is not just an economical measure, I'm sure. It means that you can never be alone long with your troubles and worries, and as such it is invaluable. I never had a strong disagreement with any roomie on tour, from Geoff Miller, who semed to spend most of his time asleep, to Henri, who hardly spends any time asleep, and Mike Hendrick, with whom I shared a homely mug of hot chocolate before bed every night.

'Of course, there are times on tour when nothing is happening, and everyone is entitled to think he might want to go home at some stage. But I am one of the lucky ones who can easily relax and read a book – I read far more on tour than at home – without feeling constantly restless.'

Touring is a part of professional cricket which has never suited everyone and never will. I have seen some players literally counting the days to the flight home. But David Gower, at present anyway, is not amongst them.

9. The Captains

Whenever cricket followers get together, it seldom takes long for the conversation to touch on one of two popular subjects: the composition and the captaincy of the current England team. As material for a quiet chat among friends, these are explosive topics – an argument is almost guaranteed to result.

But, while those outside the game might bicker for hours over their particular choice of leader, the majority of players are unanimous that there have been just two great English captains during the 1970s. One is a typically blunt, tough and astute northerner, the other a scholarly, shrewd southerner. Between them, they have captained David Gower through most of his young career.

Gower's recollection of his first meeting with Ray Illingworth is hazy. He cannot, he says, remember exactly what the Leicestershire captain said to him. 'But it would have been something short and sharp.' Illy, schooled in the stern cricket academy of Yorkshire, was never one to waste words.

Mike Brearley arrived in first-class cricket via the declining route which so often earns the scorn of those born north of the Trent – public school, followed by university.

One would have imagined them to be poles apart and, in some ways, they are. But in cricket terms they have much in common, chiefly a habit of winning matches and a technique of leadership that has commanded the undying respect of almost every player to experience it. It is never easy to assess just what makes a good cricket captain, but a fair assumption would be that a combination of all the merits in Illingworth and Brearley could create a leader as close to the ideal as the game has ever seen.

Illingworth was playing for Yorkshire while Brearley was scarcely out of short trousers and Gower had not even been thought of. So it is natural that, by the time their paths crossed, Illingworth was past his best as a player and past his most controversial days as a character.

He spent the last ten years of his playing career in charge of a Leicestershire side which reached its peak to win most of the domestic honours. When Gower broke into the side at the age of 18, in 1975, Grace Road was the centre of a minor cricket boom as the county won the Championship for the first time. Illingworth, whom many had considered a spent force when Yorkshire released him in 1968, had successfully snubbed his nose at all who had ever doubted him.

Not a visibly emotional man, nor a demonstrative one, Illy nevertheless retained a set of standards which he expected every one of his players to obey. Smartness of dress was prominent among them.

'He would periodically have a purge on the way we dressed. Quite rightly, he had very proper ideas on the appearance of his players, and would never stand for tee-shirts and jeans, or anything sloppy. At the start of the 1977 season, he was being particularly firm about clothes, and actually issued warnings to some of us about the way we were dressing to come to games. My sense of the ridiculous then came into play, and during our first away trip of the season, I decided that I would come down to breakfast in full evening dress.

'I put on dinner jacket, dress shirt, bow tie and smart strides and swanned into the dining-room of our hotel in Taunton looking the picture of elegance. It stunned Raymond for all of ten seconds, before he came out with the perfect retort – "Have you just come in, Gower?"'

'Whether he had mellowed a good deal by the time I came to know him, I could not say, but I certainly enjoyed his dry humour. He accepted the mickey-taking, and indulged in a fair amount himself.

'There was another occasion, a year later, when he again had the last word on me – only this time I hadn't made quite the same efforts at smartness.

'We were due to play a pre-season practice match against Notts at Trent Bridge, and, as Nottingham is only a 40-minute drive from Leicester, we were travelling up on the morning of the game. Not for the first time, I was a little late getting out of bed. I dressed in the dark, hurriedly put on some shoes and jumped in my car. I arrived in the dressing-room in something of a rush, said good morning and sat down. It was only when I bent to take off my shoes that I realised I had put on a black one and a brown one – and by then it was too late. Raymond had noticed it too ... "Bloody hell, Gower, what were you doing last night?" ... That was not something I was allowed to forget too quickly.

'He used to call me "Brain" because I was one of the few he could turn to in the dressing-room for help with his newspaper crossword. Every morning, he would start this crossword before he arrived at the ground, and try to finish it if we were batting, or during an interval. There were not many days when he wouldn't call me across: "Come here, Brain, have you got some ideas on this clue?"'

When Gower arrived at Leicester, his strength was an ability to play the seamers. It was only after some intensive coaching that he became proficient against spinners. His chief tutor was Illingworth. 'Raymond was a great spin bowler, there can be no doubt of that, and along with Jack Birkenshaw and the other spinners in the side, he was responsible for a great improvement in my game. The most important thing he taught me was the need to be de-

cisive against the spinners, to either play properly and completely forward, or go back on the stumps. Anything hesitant and half-way is disastrous against a bowler of his skill.'

Illingworth's reputation is that of a hard man, a captain who would not tolerate needlessly falling standards and who would generally say exactly what he thought. But his approach was not always harsh.

'If I was out cheaply, through having played a bad shot, he might sometimes have a go at me. But whereas some captains would unhesitatingly come down like a ton of bricks, Raymond would more often give me a few moments alone, then just come to me quietly and say something like: "What are you?" It was enough to make the point. We both knew what I was.

'When the team as a whole had played badly, however, it was different. If we needed a thorough rollocking, we got one. Raymond would go back to basics and tell us that if we did the simple things properly, the rest would follow. He never minced his words.

'Whatever he said always made sense. We might not have appreciated the tone of it at the time, but there was never any doubt that he knew exactly what he was talking about. I would have been very foolish to ignore anything he told me, and I feel the same way about Geoff Boycott. They came from the same background and both have a great deal to say about the game, almost all of it worthwhile.

'Raymond occasionally harked back to the early days of his career, particularly if he was complaining about our dress standards or something similar. "We'd never have got away with that when Brian Sellars was captain of Yorkshire" was one of his favourite lines. But in general terms, he was not one to yearn for the old days when the junior members of the side could not even talk to the captain – and for that, I am very thankful.

'Our semi-affectionate nickname for him was "Dial-a-moan" because of the inevitability of repercussions from his tongue when things went wrong. Like most captain-bowlers, he was also especially harsh on mistakes which affected his own bowling figures, and I remember one Sunday match episode which sounds hilarious now but seemed a nightmare at the time.

Ray Illingworth – my first captain and a considerable influence on my early career, improving both my attitude (a question of building big scores) and technique against spin bowling. I have been lucky to play under both Ray and Mike Brearley within my first five years of cricket.

'The previous week, we had dropped about four catches against Essex – I had been among the culprits – and taken a justifiable dressing-down from the skipper. Naturally enough, nobody was keen to miss one off Raymond's bowling when we went out to field against Derbyshire.

'As usual, he was bowling his eight overs very tidily, but Ashley Harvey-Walker, Derbyshire's tall all-rounder, suddenly swung one high in the air and straight towards me at that nondescript position we call "cow corner" – somewhere between deep mid-wicket and long-on. It came out of a bright, blue sky, and I caught it at about knee level. With huge relief, I hurled the ball about 30 feet in the air and looked up for the congratulations, only to see Raymond yelling at me, hands on hips: "Get the thing in, it's a no-ball!"

'Most people have heard classic tales of this happening, but I never thought it would occur when Raymond was bowling his slow off-breaks – you just don't expect him to bowl no-balls. To compound my sin, when I did return the ball it hit the stumps and ricocheted away, and the batsmen eventually picked up three runs for what I had thought to be a good catch.

'When I was next within hearing range, Illy snapped at me: "You're not a show pony, play the game properly." And, probably, I had asked for it.

'Raymond had tremendous pride in his own performance, as well as that of the team, and it was often amusing to be in the dressing-room when he came off after being dismissed. More often than not, he would claim it was the best ball of the day, or that it took off and turned off a plantain in the wicket. Once, after being out to a spinner at Grace Road, I remember him saying that he had lost the ball against the green paint of the balcony above the sightscreen ... and perhaps he did.

'None of these stories are intentionally told against him. I repeat them only to illustrate the intense competitive spirit of the man, which came through in everything he did. On the field, he had this permanent air of being in command. Even in times of trouble, he always gave the impression that he knew just what he was doing, and that everything was in hand. He was very much his own master, and enjoyed being in charge, but he would never discourage anyone from airing their views. His great philosophy was that everyone must have

the right attitude, and must show that they wanted to play for him. If he did not have confidence in someone's approach to the game, he would not pick him. I have a great deal of time for Raymond, and tremendous regard for the advice he gave me. There is no doubt that he helped to shape my career, and made me a better cricketer, with a more professional attitude.'

When Illingworth left Leicestershire to return to his native Yorkshire as team manager, Gower was preparing for his first England tour. He had already played six home Tests and was averaging more than fifty for England. But within a month of arriving in Australia, his form was causing such concern that he was summoned to Mike Brearley's Brisbane hotel room for a chat with the anxious captain.

'It was something new to me, as I had always been accustomed to just playing my game and being allowed to get on with it, and at first it felt as though I was being called before the headmaster to explain myself. But it was not like that at all, and I quickly appreciated the value of the fact that Mike was thinking about my problems.

'In the early stages of the tour, I had not made many runs, and Mike and "The Inspector" – as our manager, Doug Insole, became known after his impersonations of Inspector Clouseau at the Christmas party – were naturally keen to find out what was going wrong.

'Our meeting lasted no more than 20 minutes and was very informal, with Mike simply finding out if my attitude was right, if I was thinking enough about my game. He talked about the differences between batting in England and Australia, especially the different bounce, but we didn't come to any positive resolutions. Its major value to me was an indication of the thoroughness of our captain.

'Just like Illy, he gains the respect of us all through his self-assurance. I have seldom seen him

Mike Brearley at Adelaide, Fifth Test 1979, and wearing helmet and visor for the first time. He is very much respected by the players as a captain so no one would have appreciated his dropping himself because of his batting form, as he suggested half way through the 1978–79 Tour.

Ken Higgs succeeded Ray Illingworth as Captain at Leicester – not an easy task. He has in common with Raymond long experience in the game and still performs very effectively with the ball. He is quiet and likeable off the field, which may surprise those who only know him as an opponent.

at all ruffled on the field, and in fact he is usually relaxed enough to enjoy a joke and a laugh. He has much more humour than many people realise, and has the priceless virtue of seeing fun in himself as well as in other people.

'Mike will rarely say much to us before we take the field, other than a few comments during the final 15 minutes, just to harden our concentration for the day ahead.

'He sets fields precisely, and looks after bowlers to the extent of consulting them constantly about everything from field placings to methods of bowling at a particular batsman. To me, he is visibly monitoring things from over to over and always has a plan, but he will invariably check to make sure that his bowlers are capable of carrying it out.

'Mike loves having Ian Botham in the side, because he always wants to go on bowling. The only time a problem arises is when "Guy" is clearly not bowling well, yet still wants to carry on!

A contrast of expressions as we celebrate by posing for the cameras in the dressing-room at Adelaide having clinched a series win. Brearley and Taylor have achieved the false smiles, Miller is nearly there; Hendo knows what he really wants just then and I would have been happier munching my grapes out of camera. Bernard Thomas, in the background, looks as if he would rather not have been there either, as befits his modest 'behind the scenes' character.

'In my experience, Mike seeks the opinions of other players more freely than Raymond. Whereas Illy would always listen to anyone who offered a view, Mike actually goes out of his way to consult, always bringing in the bowler, the wicketkeeper and some of the other senior players.

'He will only become irritable in the field when people are not paying proper attention and he cannot catch their eye to make a quiet field alteration. Quite rightly, he feels that all his fielders should be constantly alert, and ready for changes.

'There was only one occasion on my first tour when I thought he was close to losing control on the field, and that was during a one-day international in Melbourne, when we gave a pretty inept performance and deservedly lost. It was unusual, on that tour, for the side to be under such pressure, and there were several players who became edgy. Mike, his disappointment showing, was among them. He is a deep thinker, but keeps those thoughts mostly private. In general, Mike is undemonstrative and he is certainly not the type either to throw a tantrum or make wild excuses when he is out. He will usually sit quietly, perhaps looking disgruntled but saying very little, then maybe he will seek confirmation of his view on how the fateful delivery behaved.

'Again, however, there was a solitary exception in Australia. It came during the Fifth Test at Adelaide and surprised me because it was so much out of character. Mike, who had been short of runs anyway, was adjudged caught behind off a delivery which, we all thought, had only brushed his shirt-sleeve. He arrived back in the dressing-room and, for two memorable minutes, the air was blue. His personal frustrations must have built up throughout the trip – none of us knew until later that he had once considered leaving himself out of the Fourth Test – and, like everyone else, he had a breaking point. That was the only time I have ever seen him react badly to being out, and one of the very few occasions when his calm exterior has been at all disturbed.

'There is nobody in the England side who has anything but respect and admiration for Mike, and there cannot be many eras when such harmony has prevailed throughout the side. Whenever there has been talk of him retiring we have wanted him to stay on, and whenever his place has been put in any jeopardy by poor batting form, we have willed him to make runs.

'If the mark of a good captain is loyalty from his players, then Mike Brearley must be among the best ever.'

10. Friends and Followers

The game of cricket spans the globe, but the social world of its players can be small, even closely-knit. Cricketers' friends, in general, tend to be other cricketers, or at least have a connection with the game. Complete outsiders are rare and, at least at first, may be treated with a certain mistrust by players well aware that theirs is a business which attracts all kinds of hangers-on.

From the simple, persistent autograph hunter to the crashing bores who will assail anyone after a pint too many, and so to the girls who linger, like stage-door theatre fans, hoping for a famous catch; to cricketers as a race, they are a handicap of the job. It is difficult to be consistently polite, undiplomatic to be rude. It is because of this that many cricketers, indeed top sportsmen in general, build up a protective wall around themselves and keep their friendships internal, almost incestual.

Gower has the equanimity to be friendly to most people, but would number few among close and valued relationships. There are naturally several at Leicester where, as one who enjoys being sociable, he mixes chiefly with those of similar mind. The Rhodesians, Brian Davison and Paddy Clift, share his sense of humour and many of his interests; Roger Tolchard, as his former landlord, is inevitably close.

Outside the confines of his county side, and of the England team with which we deal separately, he names Chris Cowdrey and Ian Gould as his most genuine friends. Cowdrey, of Kent, and Gould, of Middlesex – team-mates on a Young England tour to the West Indies, contemporaries brought closer by a shared sense of fun and appreciation of lunacy.

Officialdom, however, has never fallen easily on Gower's shoulders. There is that hint of rebellion in him which could conceivably have led to any number of clashes with authority, so it is gratifying that he feels both respect and affection for the administrators with whom he has had the closest contact. Men like Mike Turner, secretary, manager and guiding light behind Leicestershire cricket.

'I was sitting on the balcony at Grace Road during my first second team match, feeling shy and quiet, when Mike introduced himself for the first time. At that stage, he was very much like another schoolmaster to me – the approach was very similar. But I have come to know him for what he is, and I realise how fortunate we are to have a man like him in charge at Leicester. Nowadays, still like a schoolmaster, he is always telling me I should be scoring more runs for the county, an obvious enough sentiment. But he is also my protection in many ways, and an adviser in terms of what I should and should not be doing, off the field.'

England players encounter more administrators on overseas tours, when the relationship between team and management is crucial to the success of the trip. In Australia, on the 1978–79 tour, Gower and those with him were lucky . . .

'Doug Insole, as manager, showed a very dry, sharp wit, which I always found amusing. He was efficient without being too stiff and formal and in his public speaking, apart from frequent ums and ers which brought a good deal of mickey-taking from us, he regularly let his humour creep in – although it generally passed completely unnoticed by the people it was aimed at. His Christmas party fancy-dress choice was Inspector Clouseau, which was spectacular enough to win him the prize for the best costume, and also spoke volumes for that sense of humour.

*Brian Davison, who apart from his qualities as a
player, also happens to be a good friend, sharing
a similar sense of humour and many tastes, not to
mention thirsts.*

'I enjoyed his managership enormously, but while he confined himself chiefly to the administrative and political issues of the tour, Ken Barrington as assistant manager was constantly involved in the team's match preparations. The Colonel, as he is known to all, appeared to be in charge of laundry and nets – not in that order – and was always willing to give advice on any technical problems.

'He is a great one for the public relations bit and, every day just before lunch at a game, he would put on his tour blazer and announce that he was going off to do his P.R. job. Kenny is hugely popular all around the cricket world, and a great talker at that, but I am sure we will all remember him for his hilarious tribulations with the English language.

'One day when he was talking of Mike Hendrick's accuracy, he described his length as "getting the batsmen in TWOMANSLAND".

'At Newcastle, on the New South Wales coast, we were all about to leave for an evening reception, and Kenny was telling us that a cold buffet had been laid on for us ... a smorgasbord, in fact ... but the Colonel unwittingly called it "SMOG-OR-GAS-BORD", which did not sound quite right!

'Back in England several months later, the team were chatting over one of our regular pre-Test dinners and the conversation got around to shooting, a keen interest of both Mike Hendrick and Ian Botham. On the subject of rifles, Kenny enquired whether any of us had used "those HIGH-PHILO-SOPHY bullets"!

'Kenny, of course, is one of the four regular England selectors, all of whom I have a lot of time and respect for. Alec Bedser, the chairman, is the sort of man in whom I would put a great deal of trust ... even if he does keep telling us stories from his own heyday of 1946. Charlie Elliott, who was once what is politely known as a robust footballer, then a Test umpire, is the quietest of the four, a very knowledgeable man, and with interests in food and wine – he runs a hotel in Nottingham as a sideline hobby to his cricket! And then there is Brian Close, subject of endless good-natured ribbing from the players for his own unchangeable belief – carried over from his long and courageous playing career – that he could still do any job in the game.'

Outside the mainstream of cricket people, there are characters to be found on every ground in England, indeed in the world. The grounds themselves also have their own peculiar personality, and Gower is no different from any other player in having his preferences for crowds and venues. 'I am sure I must be in the majority in naming my own home ground among my favourites. I like Leicester not just because it is home, but for the playing surface and the general atmosphere which, to me, is always a friendly one.

'Away from Leicester on the county circuit, I enjoy the grounds which have marquees around them, such as Canterbury, Tunbridge Wells and the Essex grounds. It may seem that a row of tents makes no difference, but they always seem to make the atmosphere more relaxed and appealing.

'Rather perversely, I also enjoy The Oval. Many players think it is like playing inside Colditz, and I have to admit it has some bleak angles, but my affection for the place probably stems from 1978, when I could do no wrong every time I played there.

'Personal success, or the lack of it, will always influence a player's opinion about a certain venue. For that reason, I have fond memories of the Perth ground, where I scored my first hundred in Australia, and also of Lord's, for my maiden first-class century against Middlesex in 1976. There is a magic about Lord's, however corny it may sound. While I did not actually go weak at the knees, my first match there was an experience to be remembered – it gave me a great feeling to score runs on the most famous of the world's grounds. After playing there several more times, however, the novelty has disappeared and I have the common apprehensions about the so-called ridge.

'Among my other favourites are Trinidad, where the hills rise steeply and spectacularly away from the Port of Spain Oval, most of the Australian Test grounds and two more obscure places, in Kuala Lumpur – a ground called The Dog – and Vancouver, probably Canada's best-known cricket venue.

'If it came down to a straight choice of one, however, it would always have to be Leicester, if only for its characters. There is one chap called Christopher Wright who has never missed a day since I started playing. I know that for a fact, because it is impossible to miss his presence. Among the players, he is better known as "Foghorn", for reasons not difficult to guess, or "Birky's mate", because he always used to walk into the ground and announce himself loudly with a yelled: "I'm here, Jack," to Jack Birkenshaw. His constant shouting from the boundary, which he patrols for most of the day, often has the effect of a cheerleader on the rest of the crowd. His advice is never to be taken lightly, either, for he has often demonstrated a keen knowledge of the game. Ray Illingworth once said that if "Foghorn" shouted some advice from the side, which was obviously good advice, he never felt he could take it, even if it had been in his mind – the crowd would never have let him forget it. Nowadays, "Foghorn" lives in a house just outside the gates of the ground, and we always know when to expect him. The front door slams and he shouts: "I'm on my way, boys."

'I expect many grounds have a similar character, an eccentric but integral part of the place. Unfortunately, there are also a number of grounds where it is easy to find less savoury individuals. Drinking to excess has recently become a cricket problem, particularly on Sundays, and there have been a number of regrettable incidents when a section of spectators has behaved like the louts that have long hounded soccer.

'The worst such episode I have been part of was at Worcester in 1976, during our Benson and Hedges Cup quarter-final. The crowd spilled onto the pitch, most of them drunk, and there were a number of arrests which prompted captain Illingworth, quite rightly, to some strong words at the end of the game.

'As a professional player, I have to accept that the crowd are going to taunt me now and again. Providing the remarks are funny, rather than abusive, I don't mind at all and in fact I enjoy a rapport with crowds such as the Lord's full house for the World Cup final, where the West Indian contingent were in great spirits and provided a really marvellous atmosphere.

'But I do lose all sympathy and patience with individuals whose only wish appears to be to insult as harshly and obscenely as possible. There are fortunately few such people around the cricket circuit, but I have encountered my share, quite often in car parks at the end of a day's play.

'At Wellingborough, during a county game in 1979, I was fielding near the boundary when a spectator – wearing a Leicestershire tie, I am ashamed to say – directed some loud and lengthy remarks in my direction, to the effect that he did not appreciate either my absences from the county side (I had spent a good deal of time with England for the World Cup and the Tests) or, more hurtfully, what he called my lack of effort.

'Perhaps I should have ignored him completely, but I turned and replied mildly that I did try my best in every game. He took no notice at all, merely continuing with his character assassination, so at the end of the over I strolled over and told him that I did not at all mind him having a go at me, so long as he allowed me the right of reply. It probably made no impression on him, but I felt obliged to make the point. We may be entertainers, who stand up to be shot down, but we are also human and should not need to take such abuse without the opportunity to answer back.

'Every crowd around the country is different. In general, northern crowds are probably bigger and noisier and have always been more fervent in their parochialism – but nobody could accuse the Kent and Somerset crowds of recent years of much impartiality!'

Gower's age, glamorous projection and good looks make him an obvious target for the growing band of female followers the game has attracted. Cricketers, to some girls, have the charisma that was once reserved for film stars and pop singers – a phenomena that the ever-increasing television projection has much to do with. It may sound a bonus to be chased by members of the opposite sex every night, but that is not always the case:

'There are many girls who follow the game for its own sake, who have a genuine interest and in some cases, a deep knowledge. But there are also a number of hangers-on who can pester the players far more than we would like. It is human nature to react to an attractive girl, and if any young lady wants to talk to me about the game, I am quite happy to oblige. But equally, I will escape as quickly and tactfully as possible from those who only want to bore me. In general, I prefer to choose

Batting at Leicester, usually something to look forward to.

my own female company by mutual arrangement.'

There are similar problems with the thousands of youngsters whose day at cricket is incomplete unless they come away with a book full of autographs. In this case, every player accepts it as part of his responsibility to spend some time signing ... providing the approach is made at the right time and place:

'It gives me quite a kick to see a look of happiness on a kid's face when I have signed his book. But it just gives me a pain when I see mean, sour faces thrusting cigarette packets or grubby scraps of paper at me and virtually demanding that I sign "for my son/cousin/brother/friend etc.".

'If I have time, I am not in a rush and I am in a fair mood, I am always happy to sign a reasonable amount of books. But there are times, perhaps when things have gone badly or I am in a hurry to get somewhere, when it is neither possible nor desirable to stand around. So it annoys me when the boys, and sometimes their fathers, get upset if I will not sign.

'There is no escape from the autograph fiends. They are everywhere, always waiting and certainly showing a great deal of patience in many cases. But they must realise that they should not expect too much – especially those who want you to sign about a dozen pictures.

'Many send pictures through the post for me to sign and return, which is a good system until the greedy ones also enclose pictures of other players with a request that you get them to sign, too. Not very subtle, or flattering, that. They are even waiting outside the hotels during a Test match, for the players to come out on their way to the ground. That is one place I always refuse to sign, with the simple explanation that it is no different from being badgered outside my own front door – in other words, it is an invasion of privacy.'

Crowds, girls, autographs ... they are all extra demands in a world becoming rapidly more pressurised. There are times when a cricketer of international note needs to get away and relax, which is why Gower counts a lady called Hazel among his most valued friends.

Hazel is the landlady of 'The Cricketers', the pub which adjoins Leicestershire's Grace Road ground, and she has known Gower since, as a raw new recruit to the playing staff, he graduated to drinking age.

'She is known as "Dragon", but only in a very affectionate sense. She rules her pub, but produces a great, relaxed atmosphere. She stops anyone pestering the players and looks after us all with food. Above all, she takes the mickey out of us – and never lets our feet leave the ground.'

11. Australia 1979/80

Despite its early glamour and undoubted elements of romance, David Gower's marriage to cricket does not survive without moments when divorce seems the best and easiest way out. Few young players may have achieved so much, so soon, but Gower, like everyone else, is subject to the occasional rash of poor form – and the subsequent onset of depression.

Australia brought him more than his expected share of problems during England's hastily-conceived and reluctantly confirmed tour, in the winter of 1979–80. And, as will inevitably occur while the big innings grows steadily more elusive, the external pressures, which might otherwise be conquered, took him in an unpleasant grip.

It was, in every sense, an unusual tour. Kerry Packer had officially agreed to disband his World Series Cricket operation in exchange for the exclusive rights to televise top Australian cricket. But the story did not end there. A further part of the agreement involved conceding all promotion of international cricket to Packer's company who, quite naturally, then demanded the best teams and best players to promote. It was through this pressure on the Australian Cricket Board, and their consequent pleas to the cricket world in general, that England and the West Indies came to share the winter's activities down under.

The fact that the matches were shared, however, may give a false impression, for this was in no way an easy winter for the players. Quite the opposite. The schedules were arranged with the intricacies of underground timetables, and all three teams were obliged to rush around Australia with the frenzied air of a city gent permanently late for his train. The tour was conducted as much on the internal air

routes across Australia as in the cricket grounds, and the result was inevitable fatigue as the programme reached its climax in late January.

Both England and the West Indies played three Tests against Australia and, in addition, the three nations contested a one-day competition on a round-robin basis. Each team played eight matches, and as Australia were left bottom of the resultant league table, England met the West Indies in a best-of-three-match play-off for the One-day 'championship'.

By thus playing 10 One-day Internationals in various corners of the country, and splitting their priorities between these and the three Tests, England found themselves under constant pressure. Quite apart from the endless travelling, the programme ensured that players out of form or out of favour were given scant opportunity to regain confidence.

Gower held his place in the side, but at times it was a near thing. After starting the tour with one or two promising innings, he suffered an abysmal run of failures and was quite patently distressed. Those close to him realised the problem; captain Mike Brearley, among others, tried to lift Gower by means of constant company and encouragement. But he was clearly jaded and worried – until, that is, the run abruptly ended with an unbeaten 98 in the Second Test at Sydney, which briefly yet unavailingly lifted England's hopes of staying in the series. Ultimately, they were to lose that match, and with it the rubber – though not the Ashes, which the English authorities had, controversially, refused to put on offer for such a shortened series.

Gower said of his innings: 'After such a depressing run, including only three in the first innings of

this match, it came as a very welcome relief. The general opinion among the lads is that I did not start to play well until I was past 40, and certainly, up to that point, there had been a lot of playing and missing. Funnily enough, I never felt worried by that – which is generally a sign that things are going well. The people who did become frustrated by it were Lennie Pascoe and the Australian slip-fielders. Pascoe bowled very fast at times, and I got the odd one down to third man for four, either through or over the slips. They didn't seem at all pleased.

Above 'What am I doing here anyway?' Derek Randall during the First Test in Perth, December 1979.
Left Out of the doldrums and into the runs with 98 not out in the Second Test against Australia in Sydney, January 1980. Having been officially (that is by the Press) going through a bad patch with the bat, it came as a welcome relief to be in the runs again. To get to 40 required an inordinate amount of playing and missing. On the other hand there are those of my colleagues who perversely reckon that when that is happening it is normally a sign that I am playing well!

'I was left stranded on 98 by "Goose" Willis, who must be getting worried that this is becoming a habit. At Perth, in the first Test, "Goose" was again last out leaving Geoff Boycott unbeaten on 99! There were no hard feelings, though, and in fact I had erred, anyway, by taking a single off the second ball of a Dennis Lillee over and exposing "Goose" to the strike.'

But the satisfaction felt at such an end to his suffering has not entirely obliterated Gower's feelings about the tour as a whole, or his part in it. His first thought was that, coming so soon after the previous winter's full Australian series, it seemed just like a continuing routine.

'The previous tour had been a happy one, both personally and for the team as a whole. We had played well and won most of our matches, and I had been in decent form for much of the time. Even so, I think we all felt ready to come home by the time we approached the final Test. Some of the enthusiasm had inevitably waned. We were tired, rather stale and probably a little complacent as we had won the series so convincingly. Coming back to the same country so quickly made me feel that I had never been away. Apart from the four or five new faces, the routine was much the same and I don't believe I was alone in finding it more difficult to motivate myself. It was not new to me this time, and neither was it different enough from last year's tour to inject any special interest.

'This is not an excuse for failure, collectively or individually, but I do feel it is a feature of the winter worth highlighting. The pressures of playing cricket for virtually all 12 months of the year dawned on me some time ago, but are only now taking their toll. The longer I play, the more I feel that nerves play a part in my game, and I have to admit that I did not enjoy this tour as much as I would have liked.

'I would love a break, a real break of longer than the two months we get now. This might well be a personal thing, something to do with my concentration span not being as long as it should be. But I often wonder how the blokes who have been playing at this level far longer than me, cope with the endless demands, both mentally and physically.

'My batting form never settled. It was crazily varied. There were times when I felt good, yet got myself out, and others when I hardly knew where

Above Missed it. Bowled Croft 44 in the first of our One-day Internationals, Sydney 1979, which we eventually won by 2 runs after rain had reduced the West Indies' target. The black line where the off-stump should be is the television microphone aerial, placed there to pick up the 'atmosphere' of the game. For the day-night games at Sydney, the only time we used the white ball in international cricket, we also had to use the dark blue pads and gloves, supposedly as an aid to the umpires. Anything that helps the umpires must be a good thing.

Right 'Are those your teeth in the glass, Fiery?' Bob Taylor administering welcome relief during the One-day International at Brisbane in 39°C heat. That is one D. Gower under the wet towel feeling the effects, but at least we both got fifties before Messrs Haynes, Greenidge and Richards made our target seem a little insignificant.

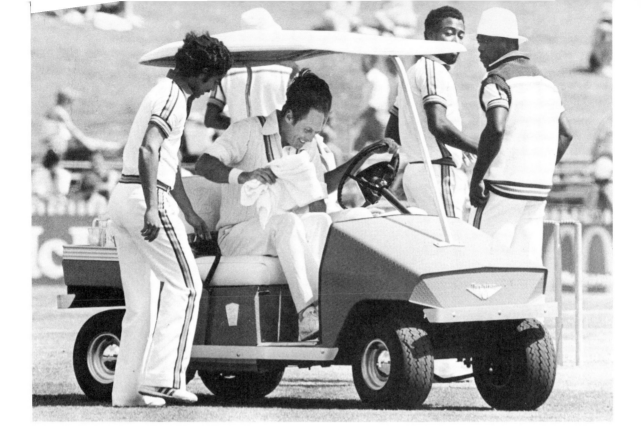

I was or what I was supposed to be doing. The difficulty is in establishing a pattern of play, when you are constantly switching from four- or five-day cricket to limited-over matches.

'By playing so much one-day cricket, it is a struggle to achieve any sort of continuity. Confidence inevitably suffers, unless you are playing as well as Geoff Boycott did on this tour. Our team works on the philosophy of not minding who makes the runs, so long as somebody does. But that does not mean that a lengthy run of failures can be excused and forgotten.

'I was particularly annoyed in the First Test at Perth. In both innings of that match, I had the impression that I was playing well, and striking the ball cleanly. Yet I was out for 17 and 23. It is times like that when I start to ask myself: "What do I do next?"

'On Boxing Day, in the One-day International, I was at the other extreme – in my mind at least. As soon as I walked to the wicket, I knew that I didn't feel right. In a way, I might just as well have turned round and walked straight back to the dressing-room. I kept losing track of my feet, I didn't know where my hands were, or where the bat was going. It was a strange and unhappy feeling, and I only hope it doesn't happen too often.

'Boycs' with the drinks buggy during the first One-day International, Sydney 1979. His dropping for that game seemed to inspire him when he came into the side for the next game and he started playing shots with a freedom not usually associated with G. Boycott, but much appreciated by the rest of the side.

'I knew, of course, that I had to do something to get out of the rut. But if I had tried to do too much, altering my game and concentrating unnaturally hard on doing things right, I knew I would destroy myself completely. It was a question of telling myself to find the balance, to go out and concentrate but to play naturally. But it got harder with every failure.'

The one complaint that appeared to be universal among players of the three nations playing in Australia was the travelling. Any normal tour of Australia can be demanding, particularly for those not keen on flying. But this one heightened the problem.

'We have a couple of nervous fliers in the side, in John Lever and Graham Stevenson. They both dread the moment of take-off in every flight, so heaven knows what they must have gone through during the course of the tour.

'Everyone in the side became sick of flying. For J.K. and Stevo, it may have been harrowing, while for the rest of us it was just a bore. There is, of course, no other way of getting around this vast country to fit the programme – so there is no point in complaining. But there were times when it all left me feeling pretty tired and unwell.

'At certain stages, the tour seemed a never-ending cycle of buses, airports and planes, packing, eating and flying. It was certainly not as relaxed as the 1978-79 tour, when we frequently spent up to two weeks in the various centres, but it is impossible to say whether, or indeed how much, it affected the performances of individuals or teams.'

Social life on any tour is important to team spirit, although some are naturally more gregarious than others. Gower, being among those who enjoy the conviviality and variety of evening life that overseas tours can provide, found things a little different this time.

'The usual routine of an evening on tour involves a drink with the opposition after play, perhaps a shower and change of clothes at the hotel, then another drink in the team room and a meal with some of the other lads. There are nights, of course, when either the team, or various individuals, are invited to parties, most of which provide a pleasant change.

'This year, having been absent from Australia for only nine months, we rediscovered some old haunts, and uncovered some new ones. Aside from the regular round, however, I broke the habit of a lifetime and went to two rock concerts, both of which I very much enjoyed – as much for the change in atmosphere and routine as anything else. I saw Graham Parker and the Rumour, who produced a lively concert which I found quite stirring, then went to see something really English in Elton John. Both the sound and the music were tremendous, and provided a memorable night.

'There are regular trips to the cinema, some of us being devotees of the silver screen, and I managed to see Monty Python's "Life of Brian", which not only gave all of us who went a lot of laughs and a fund of team jokes, but also gave me a character for the Christmas Lunch fancy dress party, which is threatening to become an annual tour tradition.

'Having gone as a cowboy the previous Christmas, this time I managed to get together a Pontius Pilate costume. With captain Mike Brearley as "The Greengrocer from Galilee", Graham Gooch as "Oliver Twist" and numerous other weird and wonderful inventions, I had plenty of scope to indulge my enjoyment of photography.

Pontius Pilate with a Pentax – inspired by Monty Python's 'Life of Brian'. Others at the Christmas Day lunch include Kenny Barrington as the Indian, Graham Gooch as Oliver Twist, complete with gruel bowl and spoon and Mike Brearley as the greengrocer from Galilee, purveyor of Jerusalem artichokes.

'It was the advent of night cricket which brought about the major change in our living style and social lives. With the matches themselves not finishing until 10.15 pm, it was usually about 11.30 by the time we had showered, dressed, shared a drink with the opposition and returned to the hotel. But, despite the hour, none of us ever felt like going to bed.

'I remember in particular our opening floodlit match, against the West Indies. Nobody had given us a chance against them – in fact, we were widely tipped, by the Australian press at least, to finish a comfortable third in the competition – but we won a very exciting match by two runs. Everyone was on a high that night – we felt we had proved something, and rammed some very premature words back at the doubters. While the adrenalin was still pumping like that, there was no way any of us felt like sleeping until about three in the morning.

'That was to be the regular pattern after these games and, while there would have been no problems if we had slept through to ten or eleven in the morning, the body clock could not adjust that quickly. I, for one, still found myself waking at my normal time, which meant I was being left desperately short of sleep.

'On one occasion, we had to be up even earlier than usual, as we were leaving for an eight o'clock flight – and that, after one of the night games and another three-in-the-morning job. This was a problem that the World Series players had to contend with for two years, and it certainly places new strains on the body, both mentally and physically.

'But, if this was the drawback of night cricket, I also found much to enjoy in the floodlit games. There was, without doubt, a different atmosphere, and being under the glare of the spotlights made me feel more like an entertainer than a sportsman.

Left This is what happens while the players are having what in this case must have been supper, in the break between innings at a day-night game in Sydney. The policy now seems to be to entertain the crowd throughout the whole day, or perhaps to provide light relief from the cricket, so that we saw exhibitions of gymnastics, volleyball, soccer and even more cricket, as well as the rock bands, during both the Test matches and the One-day Internationals. Looking at the crowd in this picture, the music does not seem to have distracted them from their dedication to slipping the amber liquid down their necks. You might have spotted from the scoreboard that England were nowhere near the SCG at the time, probably involved in a warm-up game against Combined Universities or some such opposition.

Right Peter Willey demonstrating the airborne slash against Rodney Hogg under lights at Sydney on Boxing Day 1979, a shot that Derek Randall might describe as the 'Walleroo'. During his innings 'Will' also had to contend with a firework display which left smoke drifting across the field and the sounds from the speedway next door at the showground, but he and Geoff Boycott still managed to set up an England win. Incidentally, he missed the ball this time.

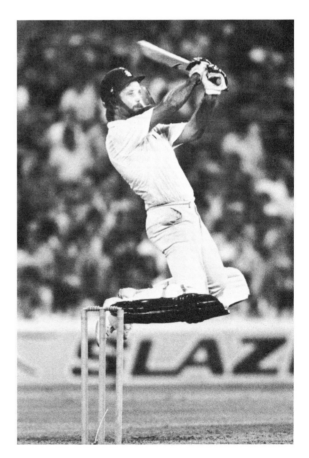

Michael Holding bowling to Mike Brearley as effortlessly as usual. 'Brears' looks to be getting himself into a good position behind the line of the ball and with a very straight backlift. Interesting to see how well the white ball shows up against the black sightscreen, something that it is impossible to consciously appreciate at the time.

'There had been a good deal of uncertainty, and different opinions, about the match conditions when we flew out. There were proposals that we should wear the striped clothing for one-day games, and this produced lengthy discussions between our management and the Australian authorities. As a side, we did not approve, because we could see no cricket reason for wearing stripes – although we would have been willing to play in a plain colour, such as the reds, yellows and pale blues used by the World Series players last season.

'Personally, I found myself getting used to the stripes after the initial distaste had worn off. Once we had played against them a few times, they seemed far more reasonable, although the cut of the clothes left plenty to be desired.

'There must be a chance that colours, or at least flashes of colour, will eventually be introduced into English cricket, just as they arrived on the tennis circuit. As long as the schemes and the extent of it is controlled with good sense, I cannot see that such an innovation will do the game any harm at all.

'The other contentious issue was the white ball. After using it in practice sessions a few times, most of us agreed it was at least equally as good as the red ball – with a couple of reservations. The wicket-keepers were having difficulty in sighting the white ball against white clothing and, for batsmen, there was occasionally a problem in picking it up as it pitched, if the wicket was one of very light colour.

'I believe there was justification for using the white ball at night, to which we agreed, and that most of the difficulties were in the individuals' minds. Psychologically, if you say to yourself that anything is new, or very different, you are bound to talk yourself into trouble. The thing to do in this case was to accept it as being just the same as before and take everything as it came.'

If the news early in the tour generally flowed from talks held off the field, more violent controversy was to follow. No sooner had the real action begun than Dennis Lillee and Ian Chappell, old adversaries of the Australian establishment, were at it again.

That Lillee is a showman, and Chappell a typically tough and sometimes graceless Australian, comes as news to nobody who has followed cricket with even a modicum of interest over recent seasons. The saving grace for both men has been the

combined virtues of courage and ability. Lillee over-
came a back injury which might have crippled the
career of a lesser man, and resumed his place at the
forefront of the world's fast bowlers. Chappell,
although never the elegant stylist which his younger
brother Greg became, was not only a superbly
combative batting technician, but a captain whom
most Australians place above any other of modern
times. Their return to the Test fold after two years
with WSC – along with other prodigals such as
Greg Chappell, Rod Marsh, Jeff Thomson and Len
Pascoe – was bound to improve the fortunes of the
hitherto toiling Australian side. Yet, although both
made telling contributions, it was their temper and
tantrums which made headlines.

*Ian Chappell – brought back to the fold for the
One-day International against the West Indies at
Sydney, December 1979, to bolster the Australian
batting, despite having been shrouded in
controversy for most of the season as a result of
trouble with umpires. Whatever else may be said,
he proved himself once again to be solid and
reliable with runs in both the one-day games and
the Test Match.*

How to get 10 minutes free television time to advertise your product. Umpires Don Weser and Max O'Connell are trying to convince Dennis Lillee that his aluminium bat is not quite the thing for a Test Match, after Mike Brearley had contended that the bat was damaging the ball. Within the next 10 minutes Greg Chappell had appeared on the field with an orthodox willow and Dennis had disappeared back into the dressing room before eventually accepting another more suitable weapon. While the negotiations dragged on, the rest of us had a 10-minute break for relaxation, as Peter Willey, Bob Taylor and Geoff Miller show in the picture.

Chappell was serving a three-match suspension for swearing at an umpire even as the England team arrived. His return coincided with South Australia's fixture with England ... and more trouble.

'Ian Botham was bowling when Chappell came in, and his second ball to him was an intended bouncer which did not get up very high. Chappell was ducking slightly when the ball hit him on the side and deflected down to fineleg. The batsmen went through for a run, but the umpire signalled that the ball was dead because Chappell had neither played a shot nor, in his opinion, taken evasive action. "Chappelli" had a point, and may even have been right. But he over-reacted in a fairly unimportant situation, throwing down his bat and getting very heated.

'There are times when each of us feels deprived by an umpire, but at any level of cricket, it is a paramount rule that one must accept the decisions – and "Chappelli" made it very obvious that he had no intention of accepting it. It did him no good, either on that issue or in his innings, because he was probably still thinking about the previous incident when "Both" bowled him another bouncer and he was caught behind.'

Lillee was called before the disciplinary committee after the First Test, for an episode of histrionics concerning his revolutionary aluminium bat. And it was perhaps not entirely cynical to suggest that he obtained a very satisfying degree of publicity for his venture ...

'In that sense, the incident worked rather well for him. The metal bat was a business scheme for Dennis and, as such, any publicity has to be of value.

'There were a number of side-issues, however, much the most significant of which was that the ten minutes which were lost while the arguments raged could have been critical at the end of the match. No time was added on, of course, for the minutes occupied by Dennis debating the issue with Mike Brearley and the umpires, then marching off the field and back again before throwing the bat away. And I wonder if he might have felt a little mortified if we had managed to hold out through the last hour of the fifth day with, say, nine wickets down.

'As things turned out, the game was not that tight, but I don't believe even his own team-mates supported him on the issue.

'There was a humorous side to the incident, too. When Dennis came in to bat, there was a sense of anticipation amongst us. We could see that he was holding the aluminium bat – it is thinner and straighter than the customary bat and has a squarish handle – and we were all curious to see what would happen. Ian Botham was bowling, and the first one that Dennis hit properly came off the bat with a loud clang. Most of us couldn't stop ourselves laughing.

'It was, however, a regrettable thing to happen during a Test match. No player should be able to delay a match for that long by such militant methods. But I was left wondering if there is a future for the metal bat.

'When I picked it up in the dressing-room, I was not impressed by the balance or feel of the thing. But if it can be perfected, and is found to work without damaging the ball, then it could be a godsend for clubs and schools who have not got the money to continually replace normal wooden bats. However, I can appreciate that the Lawmakers would have to think hard and long before allowing a bat to be made of any new material which could alter its whole performance and change the character of the game.'

Dennis Lillee First Test at Perth 1979, bowling as aggressively as ever, if perhaps not always as quickly. DKL thoroughly deserved his award as 'Player of the Series'.

Through all the highs and lows of an extraordinary winter, Gower's chief concern was quite naturally his own contribution to the team's performance. But he spared a good deal of sympathy for those squad members who did not even get the chance to prove their worth.

'Take John Lever, for instance. All he had done, until the last two one-day matches in the group

Above Whatever you do, do not suggest to Peter Willey that helmets should be banned for fielders. In the Perth Test in 1979 Bruce Laird has swept Geoff Miller full-bloodedly and caught Peter on the part of the visor covering the ear, hard enough to cut him behind the ear and require stitches. Bob Taylor and Mike Brearley as well as the batsman can obviously feel the pain, if not quite as acutely as 'Will'.
Left Greg Chappell hooking at Perth during the First Test 1979, a shot he frequently used and mostly well, although it cost him his wicket more than once against the West Indies. Early in the tour he had to carry the Australian batting and proved our major obstacle. At least with Ian Chappell's inclusion some of the pressure on Greg was relieved. The unemployed slips are Boycott and Miller.

competition, was bowl without much success in a couple of insignificant three- and four-day games. Apart from that, his duties entailed bowling in the nets, pouring the drinks and coming on for the occasional fielding stint as substitute. It was no way to build confidence.

'Everyone in the side realises what a fine tourist "JK" is, and also appreciates that he is a very good bowler ... but he must have begun to doubt it himself! It was the fault of no-one, of course, but simply that the tour was constructed in such a way that prevented team experiments.

'There were four or five players trying to keep happy and fit with hardly any match practice at all – and it is when things get like that, that a tour seems long and home seems welcoming.'

Gower, as has been said throughout this book, constantly belies the often portrayed image of a rather casual, even lazy young batsman who thinks little about the game. In fact, he thinks very deeply, worries about his own contribution and the team's future, and is constantly concerned with his own security.

There are many thousands of young boys in England who would unhesitatingly change places with Gower, and, of course, his life holds the glamour and excitement which few other careers could match. He had come a long way by the age of 22 but he was not blind to the pressures and the pains of professional cricket. Not blind, either, to the fact that he does, indeed, have time to spare.

Appendix of Statistics

David Gower in Test Cricket

1978 v Pakistan

1st Test	c Miandad b Sikander	58
(Edgbaston)		
2nd Test	b Iqbal Qasim	56
(Lord's)		
3rd Test	lbw b Sarfraz	39
(Leeds)		

1978 v New Zealand

1st Test	run out	111
(The Oval)	c Howarth b Cairns	11
2nd Test	c Cairns b Boock	46
(Trent Bridge)		
3rd Test	c Wright b Boock	71
Lord's)	c Congdon b Bracewell	46

1978/79 v Australia

1st Test	c Maclean b Hurst	44
(Brisbane)	not out	48
2nd Test	b Hogg	102
(Perth)	c Maclean b Hogg	12
3rd Test	lbw b Dymock	29
(Melbourne)	lbw b Dymock	49

(Australia continued)

4th Test	c Maclean b Hurst	7
(Sydney)	c Maclean b Hogg	34
5th Test	lbw b Hurst	9
(Adelaide)	lbw b Higgs	21
6th Test	c Wright b Higgs	65
(Sydney)		

1979 v India

1st Test	not out	200
(Edgbaston)		
2nd Test	b Ghavri	82
(Lord's)		
3rd Test	lbw b Kapil Dev	0
(Leeds)		
4th Test	lbw b Kapil Dev	0
(The Oval)	c Reddy b Bedi	7

1979/80 v Australia

1st Test	c Marsh b Lillee	17
(Perth)	c Thomson b Dymock	23
2nd Test	b G. Chappell	3
(Sydney)	not out	98
3rd Test	lbw b Lillee	0
(Melbourne)	b Lillee	11

Test Record (up to end of Australia visit, February 1980)

Matches	Inns	N.O.	Runs	H.S.	Ave	100	50
19	30	3	1259	200*	46.63	3	6

David Gower in Test Cricket

Career figures for Leicestershire, 1975-1979
(first-class cricket only)

Year	1975	1976	1977	1978	1979	Total
Matches	3	7	24	11	12	57
Inns	5	13	33	17	21	89
N.O.	0	4	2	2	3	11
Runs	65	323	720	405	602	2115
H.S.	32	102*	144*	61	98	144*
Ave	13.00	35.88	23.22	27.00	33.44	27.11
100	0	1	1	0	0	2
50	0	1	3	1	6	11
Catches	2	4	8	5	5	24

* Not out

Landmarks

1974/75	Toured South Africa with England Schools
1975	County debut for Leicestershire
1976	Maiden county century v Middlesex (Lord's)
1976	Toured W. Indies with England Young Cricketers
1977	Awarded County Cap by Leicestershire
1978	England Test debut v Pakistan (Edgbaston)
1978	Named 'Young Cricketer of the Year' by Cricket Writers
1978	Named among five 'Wisden Cricketers of the Year'
1978	Maiden Test century v New Zealand (The Oval)
1978/79	Toured Australia with England
1979	Maiden Test double-century v India (Edgbaston)
1979/80	Toured Australia and India with England